W9-AVT-094

Get to the Point

. . . .

How To Say What You Mean and Get What You Want

. . . .

Andrew D. Gilman and Karen E. Berg

KENDALL/HUNT PUBLISHING COMPANY
4050 Westmark Drive   Dubuque, Iowa 52002

Dedication

Get To The Point *is dedicated to our families,
consultants and clients, who have supported us and
helped us shape our philosophy and communication techniques.
It is also dedicated to our many years of partnership.*

Originally published in 1989 by Bantam Books,
a division of Bantam Doubleday Dell Publishing Group.

Copyright © 1995 by Andrew D. Gilman and Karen E. Berg

Library of Congress Catalog Card Number: 95-75396

ISBN 0-7872-2232-1

Printed in the United States of America
10   9   8   7   6   5   4

Table of Contents

The Five-Minute Guide to this Book

A high proportion of American adults view the prospect of speaking in public as quite literally a *fate worse than death*.

Several years ago, in a now-famous study, a market research organization conducted a poll on the question, "What do you fear most?" The results were included in *The Book of Lists*. As you might expect, "heights" was high on the list, along with "financial problems," "flying," "serious illness," and "death." But topping the list — the number one fear — was "speaking before a group."

Yet this is a prospect more and more of us face every day. We may be living in the "electronic communications age," when information is transmitted via computers, telephones, cellular phones, pagers, videoconferencing, memos and face-to-face meetings. But the operative word here is communication. For while electronics make many kinds of communication possible, in *most situations* the *most effective* means of communication is human being to human being.

⊛ ⊛ ⊛ ⊛ ⊛ ⊛

It is in direct, face-to-face presentations that we have the best opportunity to get our message across — to get to the point.

⊛ ⊛ ⊛ ⊛ ⊛ ⊛

We'd like to make it clear at the outset that we're not talking about formal speeches. Very few of us ever need to give speeches. Rather, we are referring to the relatively short and informal talks with clearly defined objectives that take place most often in a work-related context. Although there are different types of talks, each with unique goals, for our purposes let's simply call them *presentations*.

Presentations — and therefore presentation skills — are more important in the business world than they have ever been before. Every passing day swells the ranks of people who need to be able to present effectively in order to do their jobs well. In particular, presentation skills are vital to any person who ever has to *sell, persuade, motivate, inform,* or *represent.*

✸ ✸ ✸ ✸ ✸

Like it or not, it is often in the five- to fifteen-minute presentation that customers, competitors, peers, potential employers, bosses, and regulators make decisions on ideas and concepts you have been working on for months or years. So, we believe it is critical that you match your communication skills with your other professional and personal credentials.

✸ ✸ ✸ ✸ ✸ ✸

OUR BOTTOM LINE

The purpose of *Get to the Point* is to teach those skills. If you read this book and follow our program, it will reduce your presentation anxiety to a manageable level. (In fact, it may actually make the experience almost enjoyable.) But more to the point, it will *make you a better presenter/communicator.* These skills will work for business presentations, meetings, media interviews, computer-assisted presentations, witnessing, job interviews, and social settings.

OUR BOTTOM LINE II OR WHAT'S NEW IN THIS BOOK?

Since we first wrote *Get to the Point* in 1989, several key changes have occurred in the world at large, and specifically in the business world — changes that affect the way we communicate. For one, all of us are busier. We have more to do and less time to do it. The business world has gone through several downsizings, with fewer managers required to do more work. Thus, there is less time to focus, prepare, and rehearse for communications. The world is also getting smaller and smaller, with nearly every business adding an international flair. Computers and technology are playing an even greater role in our lives, with virtually seamless movement from home, to office, to travel. More and more Americans are computer literate and now proficient at programs for word processing, spreadsheets, and graphics. The media continues to grow in importance, with most managers having opportunities to communicate via videoconferences, and also with trade press and the general media.

We've done our best to reflect these changes in this book. Our commitment to readers and clients is to stay as current as possible with trends in communications.

WHO DO WE THINK YOU ARE?

From our vantage point as communications consultants and trainers, the audience for this book is quite broad. A few examples may suffice to indicate the range: the book editor presenting the spring list to the publishing house sales force; the advertising account manager outlining an ad campaign for a prospective client; the engineer instructing a manufacturing team; the consultant updating a client on project status; the law associate briefing a senior partner on research for an important case; the executive talking with business or trade press; the corporate manager talking via videoconference to colleagues a continent away; the college graduate interviewing for a new job; the unhappy consumer complaining to a store manager; all these — and many more — fall with-in our definition of *presenters*. All of these need to know how to get to the point.

WHO ARE WE?

Karen Berg and Andrew Gilman are the principals of CommCore, a New York and Washington, D.C.-based communications consulting firm. We prepare business people and public officials for the full range of communications challenges. Among others, our clients include AT&T, Kraft/General Foods, New York Medical College, NYNEX, Morgan Stanley, Bell Atlantic, Very Special Arts, Revlon, Pfizer, Hoffmann-La Roche, IBM, Johnson & Johnson, Greystone Realty and the China External Trade Development Council. Most of our work involves teaching the specific skills we will discuss in this book: how to make better, stronger presentations.

We also prepare clients for media appearances — from trade and consumer press to radio and television interviews, including programs such as *60 Minutes* and *20/20*. We frequently prepare expert witnesses for sworn testimony before congressional committees, administrative agencies, and public utility commissions. Other seminars we offer include sales skills, stress management, writing, and crisis communications.

GETTING AHEAD

How important are presentation skills? In today's competitive business world, highly developed presentation skills add up to a bankable career advantage that you won't want to be without.

* * * * * *

The ability to make successful presentations has become a prerequisite in business.

* * * * * *

A generation ago, the ability to make a skillful presentation was a nice plus for a manager, but back then it was the possession of technical job-related skills that helped you get ahead. Today, things have changed; today the edge goes to those with highly developed communication skills. Because while technical skills are important, communication is ultimately what business is about.

It makes sense, doesn't it? Put yourself in the position of an employer. Assume you are considering two equally qualified candidates, with good references and experience. Which one would you hire? Probably the one with the better communications skills, because the one who is better able to communicate the needs and demands of the job is more likely to do the job successfully.

Presentation skills are becoming a direct link to promotion and success. In many companies today, good verbal presentation ability is a *specific requirement* for advancement. In companies such as Pfizer and Johnson & Johnson, a significant factor in personnel evaluations is an employee's ability to present well. In fact, one executive at General Electric told us why he came to work on his presentation skills: "My manager, the division vice president, told me what it would take to get any higher up the ladder. He said, 'You have the right training, have made the right moves within the company, and have proven yourself by your performance. How you look, act, and talk will determine where you go from now on.'"

TRAINING: A COMPETITIVE EDGE

Every person brings natural strengths and weaknesses to the challenge of public presentation; each of us instinctively handles some aspects well and, after practice, will learn from experience. But given the pace and intensity of life today, few of us can afford to rely on our natural gifts or the accumulation of experience to acquire this edge.

Consider an analogy: A tennis player gets ahead by learning to hit the ball accurately and assertively, by learning to reach any ball and return it authoritatively. That's how points are made.

A weekend player can rely on natural talent plus a few pointers from fellow players. After all, in the long run there is rarely money or a career at stake. A *professional* tennis player, however, learns winning skills by training with a professional coach virtually every day, until these skills become second nature.

It's no different for a communicator: The ability to serve a clean and assertive message, to field a challenge or question from any position and play it back with strength and authority, is the essence of effective public presentation.

With the competitive edge professional training provides, you can learn to make your points — and that means selling your organization, your products, your services, your point of view with confidence.

That's what *Get to the Point* is all about.

THE TRIANGLE OF PERSUASION

Picture a triangle. At one angle, there is the word "You"; at another, "Audience"; at the third, "Message." All three of these elements operate in any presentation. The key to success is enhancing each one of these elements so that as each factor interacts with another — somewhere in the middle of the triangle — your message is clearer, more focused and persuasive.

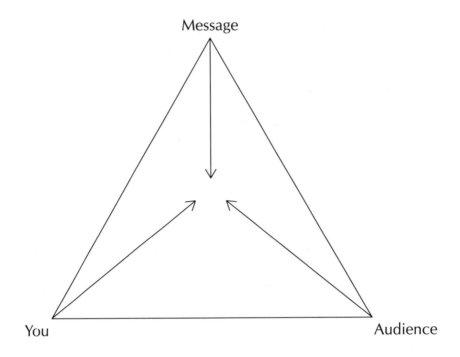

BOTTOM LINE — AGAIN

Let us reiterate our goal. (As you will shortly see for yourselves — we don't mind repeating ourselves — it's a sound communications strategy.) If you acknowledge the importance of making presentations and you feel your skills could be stronger, *Get to the Point* will improve your skills. If you're a beginner, *Get to the Point* will turn you into a capable, confident presenter. If you're already experienced, *Get to the Point* will make you better.

As skilled presenters and communicators, we use the techniques we teach nearly every day. And they work — for us and for our clients.

Our wide experience allows us to teach you basic skills of presentation making and to train you in advanced skills as well. We'll explore numerous situations that we and our clients have faced — print and media interviews, legal and legislative testimony, panel discussions, media appearances, meetings, job interviews, crisis situations, and more. As your presentation powers grow, *Get to the Point* will continue to assist you.

CAVEAT

We must point out that *Get to the Point* is not a quick, magical program. For it to work, you have to work. And the *harder* you are willing to work, the *better* it will work.

THE CAPSULE VERSION

In keeping with our goal-oriented approach, we want to give you the basics of the *Get to the Point* program. Here's our approach to presentation making, reduced to its bare essentials.

- Know your audience.
- Decide on your bottom-line message or action plan and say it early. If possible, pull in your audience with a strong attention getter.
- State your supporting points with clarity, focus, and emphasis.
- Anticipate listeners' questions and concerns.
- Make your points again while answering questions.
- Use Signal Words to alert your listeners to key points in your presentation.

BACKGROUND

Here is some of the research that forms the foundation of our program, which will be discussed in the chapters that follow.

Ebbinghaus. Much of the basis for our approach to communications is drawn from research about retention, the ability of the human mind to remember what it has taken in. The basic facts are condensed from the work of Hermann Ebbinghaus, pioneer researcher on the psychology of human memory, around the turn of the century.

Ebbinghaus' research tells us that the typical listener will forget 40 percent of what he or she has heard during a presentation within half an hour. By the end of the day, 60 percent will be gone. A week after hearing a presentation, the average listener *retains* only about 10 percent of what was said.

Our whole approach is designed to maximize retention; to increase that 10 percent. To put it another way, if your audience will only remember 10 percent of your content, how can you make it the 10 percent you want? One key to improved retention is *focus*. Clearly focused messages are easier to remember than unfocused ones. We have a lot to say about focusing on your overall purpose, on your specific point, and on your audience.

The other keys to retention are *repetition* (the more frequently a message is heard, the more likely it is to be remembered) and *proximity* (the more recently a message is heard, the better it will be remembered). We are great believers in the rule for verbal communications propounded by the late journalist, Edward R. Murrow: "Tell 'em what you're gonna tell 'em. Tell 'em. Then tell 'em what you told 'em." In keeping with this principle, you'll find us deliberately repeating ourselves quite a bit.

Nonverbal aspects of verbal communication. More recent research by Albert Mehrabian on the nonverbal elements of communication tells us that words are not the whole message. Far from it: One important study concludes that only 7 percent of interpersonal communication is traceable to words; about 55 percent is the result of facial expression and other body language; and the remaining 38 percent comes from "paralanguage," or how we use our voices. We give extensive coverage to the nonverbal elements of delivery: physical gestures, eye contact, vocal inflection, and phrasing.

Other research tells us that presentations are more persuasive if they are supported by *visual materials*. We have a lot to say about the selection, design, and use of visual aids.

A CHAIN IS ONLY AS STRONG . . .

To draw these elements together — focus, repetition, body language, use of visuals — is to create powerful communication. There is no single key to better and more convincing presentations. Think of these elements as a chain forged from a series of links, and only as strong as the weakest of them.

ONE LAST TIME

Get to the Point offers you a wealth of practical suggestions. We hope you'll read the book, and say, "Ah-ha! That makes sense. This will help me make my point more clearly and more directly."

We designed the book to be flexible. If you have a five-minute presentation to give this afternoon, go right to our Quick Points section on the Talking Memo in Chapter 25. If you have a fifteen-minute presentation to give tomorrow, see our Quick Point 'In-Flight' Presentation Writing technique. If you already know how to organize a presentation, skip to Chapter 8 on visuals; if you are familiar with the use of visuals, you might want to concentrate on Q & A (question and answer) techniques, covered in Chapter 10. Once you've mastered all the fundamentals, you will want to learn our advanced techniques. Whatever aspect of presentation making you want or need to improve, we can help.

But the book will work only as hard as you are willing to work. If you follow our suggestions and put in the time, you'll make better presentations. It's that simple.

Get to the Point is a complete presentation training program. And it works. We know because we teach it, day in and day out, to people whose success proves it.

Quick Reference Summary

- Public speaking is the number one fear of Americans.
- Face-to-face verbal presentations are the most effective way to make your point to others.
- This book will reduce public-speaking fear and make you an expert presenter.
- Presentation skills are a requirement for success in business, vital to anyone who ever has to sell, persuade, motivate, inform, or represent.
- Our training will help you improve your skills quickly and dramatically.
- The basic components of strong presentation making are:
  — Know your audience; anticipate their needs.
  — Know your bottom-line message and say it early.
  — Anticipate listeners' questions and answer them during the presentation.
  — Make your key point again in a summary statement.

- The typical listener forgets 40 percent of what he or she has heard in the first half hour; 60 percent by the end of the day; 90 percent after a week.
- Clarity, focus, and repetition help build listener *retention.*
- Visual aids help increase comprehension and retention.
- How you look, move, and speak can outweigh the content of what you say.
- If you follow the program and *do the work,* this book can teach you the basics and the fine points of presentation making, turning you into a confident presenter.

We also want you to let us know how this book works for you. We're always looking for success stories, or where clients have overcome a communications challenge. Since we're active consultants, we keep up to date on new techniques and ideas. Give us a call or send a question to:

Karen Berg
CommCore International
156 Fifth Avenue
Suite 701
New York, NY 10010
212-206-1003
212-727-9126 fax

Andrew Gilman
CommCore Communications
888 17th Street, NW
Suite 1200
Washington, D.C. 20006
202-659-4177
202-331-0679 fax

Game Plans:
The Audience Profile

Knowing your audience is the first and most crucial step in giving a presentation. You'll always have an audience, but each audience is different. Your content, style, and delivery will vary depending on the group.

• • • • • •

There is a distinction between "speaker-centered" and "audience-centered" messages.

• • • • • •

Speaker-centered messages are the points that the presenter wants to make. They reflect the speaker's perceptions and needs. Audience-centered messages reflect the needs, concerns, attitudes, beliefs, and understanding of the people addressed.

Skilled presenters understand that messages need to be audience centered and design their presentations accordingly. This does not mean that their messages are not speaker-centered, but that they strike a balance. What the audience needs to hear and what you have to say are both important. Therefore, the most powerful message is one that integrates the two. This approach to message building is fundamental to the art of *getting to the point*. And this is true no matter what audience you are addressing.

CASE STUDY: In 1985, a then upstart company, MCI, played David to the communications industry's Goliath, AT&T. MCI brought suit for antitrust violations. Like David, MCI won, but this victory was muted in the subsequent damage suit. While subsequent telecommunications history may have softened this blow, the billions of dollars sought by MCI ended up as an award of only millions.

After a trial in Chicago in 1985, a member of the jury commented that one important factor in determining the amount of damages was that the precise meaning of crucial MCI evidence was *"never made clear to the jury."* (Emphasis added.) Had the jury clearly understood MCI's complex statistical argument, he implied, the damages could have been significantly higher.

The MCI attorneys apparently had fallen into a classic communications trap: not identifying and addressing their real audience. Instead of speaking to the jury in *language they could understand,* they were drawn into an intricate, high-tech statistical debate with the opposing counsel. MCI won the debate, but the practical, dollars-and-cents cost of their failure to correctly identify and speak to their audience might have been as high as billions of dollars.

The jury in the MCI case undoubtedly suffered from the MEGO ("My Eyes Glaze Over") Syndrome. MEGO strikes any audience when the information is either too technical or not focused on the audience's needs. While the people are still physically in the room, their eyes begin to take on a "not there" look. The cure for MEGO is usually shorter, more energetic, audience-centered presentations.

THE AUDIENCE PROFILE

To create audience-centered messages, the speaker must know the audience — their knowledge, needs, concerns, interests, attitudes, beliefs, and in many cases even their personalities. The *better* the speaker knows them, the more finely tuned his or her messages can be. That is why the first step in preparing for any presentation is an accurate and detailed audience profile. It is the strategic foundation for a successful presentation. It's your game plan.

Defining your audience is parallel to the process a football team goes through in preparing for a game. In the big leagues, it's not enough to be good; the winning edge comes from knowing your opponent's game as well as you know your own. Professional football teams hire scouts to watch other teams. They analyze each opposing player's strength, speed, stamina, and spirit. Based on this information, the coaches work out a game plan that adapts their team's strengths to best meet the challenge of the opposing team. That's what the audience profile does for a presenter.

This preparation is both offensive and defensive. In football, the goal of the offense is tailoring plays to gain yardage and score points. In a presentation, the objective is tailoring *messages* to make your point. In football, the job of the defense is turning back challenges mounted by the opposition. In a presentation, similarly, the speaker's goal is to meet any challenges or resistance from the audience, usually by anticipating and answering questions.

Questions, questions. Doing an audience profile is a process of questioning. Questions shed light on different facets of your audience.

If you know your audience personally, for example, your questions will relate to the power levels, specific turfs, subject matter expertise, and personal idiosyncrasies of individual participants. We'll discuss presentations to specific audiences later. For the moment, we'll stick with general audiences.

If your audience is a complete unknown, you really need to start at the beginning.

Question:

Who's going to be there; who are *these people?*

Basic demographic information can give you the overview that serves as the background for a more detailed picture. Basics include:

- Age
- Sex
- Income level
- Occupation or professional status
- Political affiliation
- Ethnic identity

＊ ＊ ＊ ＊ ＊ ＊

Gather basic audience profile information even if you think you know it. Assumptions can get you into trouble.

＊ ＊ ＊ ＊ ＊ ＊

Don't assume you know this basic information — find someone who does. If you are an invited speaker, for example, and you're going in cold, the contact person in the organization who issued the invitation would be a logical source to tap.

CASE STUDY: Not long ago, an editor from a major metropolitan newspaper was invited to fill in at the last minute for the scheduled speaker at a weekly luncheon gathering of public relations professionals. The editor knew that the people who usually attended these meetings were entry-level and junior account exec types and therefore thought it wasn't a very important event. Her talk was aimed at such an audience; it had the tone of wisdom talking to inexperience and could be summarized along the lines of, "You people will have to learn to write a proper press release if you want to get along with us."

What she didn't know was that the speaker she replaced was a very important industry figure. As a result, the crowd that day actually contained a lot of executive vice presidents and CEOs; people who had the power to decide when she got a story — or if she got one at all. They were not accustomed to being addressed in this tone, nor was the message appropriate to this group. Simply taking the time to ask the basic audience profile questions could have avoided this debacle.

As the story shows, accurate audience identification will influence things as fundamental as your choice of subject matter or content.

Question:
What do you want to tell these people;
what do they need to hear?

Just as you would design one sort of message for CEOs and another for assistant account executives, you would want to present different kinds of material to a consumer watchdog group than you would to the Lions Club. And the Lions Club in Cincinnati will be different from a similar organization in Philadelphia. The same holds true in other settings.

Getting inside their "heads." The goal of the basic audience profile is understanding the audience's point of view and providing answers to the questions everyone carries around in the back of their mind:

- "So what?"
- "Who cares?"
- "What's In It For Me?" (WIIFM)

A good way of getting the answers to these questions is to focus on the audience's relationships.

Question:
What is the audience's relationship to itself?

What defines this particular group? What is their common thread? What issues, attitudes, concerns, or backgrounds forge this diverse collection of individuals into a unified group?

These questions will tell you where the group's attention will be focused, providing you with an accurate index of your audience's interests and concerns.

Question:
What is your relationship to the audience?

Are they customers? Colleagues? Your boss (or bosses)? Stockholders? Neighbors? Potential followers? Or simply fellow citizens? Are you appearing as an authority? An informer? An advocate? An apologist?

Question:
What do you have in common with your audience?

What natural points of alliance do you see? What threads can you weave into your presentation that will continually reaffirm those connections, binding you together and counteracting any natural antagonisms? The range of possibilities is quite broad. It might be goals — personal, professional, social, or political; interests — common or opposing; a business or occupation; an affiliation; a skill; or an occasion (such as a retirement party or a sales awards banquet).

Question:
How knowledgeable would you expect this group to be in your area of expertise; what level of interest can you anticipate?

Answers to these questions can provide clues to the appropriate *depth* of your presentation. Gauging depth can be important. You certainly don't want to talk down to people; it's deadly. Nor do you want to talk over their heads.

CASE STUDY: A client of ours who manages a major company's research laboratory took a group of new employees on an orientation tour of the facility, supplying a running commentary about blood chemistry, hemoglobin, and platelet research. When the tour was finished, he asked if anyone had any questions. One man raised his hand and asked, "What's a platelet?"

Question:
What are the potential areas of conflict and confrontation with the audience?

In spite of tailoring a message based on an audience profile, nearly every presenter raises issues that may be possible sources of dispute. Every message has the potential for conflicts, and identifying these is the second crucial goal of the audience profile process.

The strongest presentation is one in which you, the presenter, invite questions, but in many situations a question and answer session may be mandatory. If you haven't anticipated the inevitable tough questions and have not prepared good answers, the strength of the presentation may be completely undermined. We will discuss this more fully in Chapter 10.

Here's a final question you should ask before any presentation where the speaker is unfamiliar with the attendant conditions.

Question:
Are there any special circumstances surrounding this presentation?

The question about circumstances is really about anticipating your audience's frame of mind, and together with consideration of your relationship to the audience, bears on the tone your presentation takes. It's always worth a discreet question to your contact person on the day of the presentation: "Is there anything going on that I should know about?" If the president of the foundation died of a heart attack earlier in the week; if the company's local plant recently released massive amounts of toxic chemicals into the local water supply; if the sales force just landed a substantial government contract for portable computers; these are things you need to know *before* you make your presentation. This kind of knowledge can spare you the embarrassment of being lighthearted or flippant in somber circumstances or will enable you to focus on positive developments.

THE INSIDE VIEW

The approaches to the audience profile we have outlined thus far are applicable primarily to public presentations. For what we call internal presentations — those that take place within a company or organization — the focus is generally quite different. The principle is the same, but there are two significant ways in which internal presentations differ from public ones.

First, you are much more likely to be working with a pre-established agenda; the subject matter is usually determined by others. As a result, goals are likely to be clearly defined and results easy to evaluate: Did you accomplish your purpose? Was your budget approved? Was your task force recommendation accepted? Did you get authority to hire the five new people you need?

Second, since companies are hierarchically structured, a specific focus of the message must be persuading key people and placating others. Individual personalities must be taken into account during preparation. The audience will be a complex mixture of human factors: people with a vital stake in the outcome and those with none; staunch supporters and inveterate opponents; friends, mentors, protegés, enemies, potential allies, and everything in between.

Personality profile. Your preparation for an internal presentation should profile each important audience member — as a personality, and in terms of job function and power. Here are some of the questions you should consider.

Questions:
Who are the key people you have to persuade in order to accomplish your goal?

Have you developed a WIIFM (what's in it for me — pronounced "wiffum") for each of these people?

What personal idiosyncrasies or habits might affect your presentation?

For example, if there is a key person who has a reputation for arriving late for meetings or leaving early, do you arrange the agenda to accommodate that person?

Focusing on the individual. What are the overriding personal concerns of each key person?

Questions:

Who's bottom line-oriented; who goes for the broad overview?

Who's concerned with pricing, timing, human resources, environmental issues?

How do you and your message relate to any or all of these concerns?

Rather than compete with these players, can you find a way to form a tennis doubles team and play on the same side of the net?

Question:

From whom can you expect opposition as a matter of course?

Is there a tough-minded executive who likes to grill *everybody?* Is there someone who just doesn't like you?

Question:

From whom can you expect real (substantive, as opposed to personal) opposition?

Who is likely to genuinely disagree with your plan? This part of the profile is essentially no different from that for public presentations.

Questions:

What are your answers to this opposition?

With whom might you build alliances before presentation time?

Who among the participants is important enough to require acknowledgment (usually a special WIIFM message), even though not a key player in this scenario?

That is, are there any VIPs present whose feathers would be ruffled if they were left out of the discussion despite the fact that they don't have a decision-making role in the issue at hand?

Also consider the organization's political climate of the moment (who is receptive to particular types of moves, projects, or approaches, and who is not) and the organizational "culture" (in this connection, primarily a question of what kinds of positions or stances can be taken by people in different levels of the organizational power structure without violating the group sense of "good form").

If you have any doubts about the political mood, sample opinion in one-on-one sessions before the meeting. If the climate is clearly hostile to the kinds of ideas and approaches you wish to set forth, you may want to reconsider your position for now.

Sensitivity to "culture" can help you avoid the pitfall of calling attention to yourself in the wrong ways — of offending higher-ups by overstepping your position. The same awareness can guide you in making your point without violating corporate canon.

Here are two real-life examples that demonstrate the value of a detailed audience profile for internal presentations:

CASE STUDY 1: Twice a year the sales force of a major U.S. corporation gathers for a meeting with corporate management for a review. Sales figures are discussed, as are projections and goals for the rest of the year. At this meeting, management asks questions, seeks clarifications and explanations, probes, examines, and picks at details. It's potential "on the carpet" time for the sales reps, and they have to be prepared to deal with any matter the brass wants to raise — and try to come out looking good.

Also on the agenda are any problems, suggestions, complaints, or special projects that sales personnel want to bring before corporate management.

From a tactical point of view, the salespeople have three goals at these meetings:

- To present their track record as positively as possible
- To anticipate and develop answers to questions and problems managers are likely to raise
- To create a favorable climate for their own agenda

Sales personnel felt they could make considerably better use of these meetings, so they invited us to help them prepare. We held a two-day planning and training session in which every part of the presentation agenda was examined carefully.

One of our real skills is helping people see the significance of information they already have in their heads — such as the company's sales figures — and shaping such information into messages aimed at particular persons and their interests. To do this effectively, it is necessary to understand the people and interests at which the messages are aimed — to do an audience profile.

Accordingly, we spent 10 percent of the entire preparation time — over an hour and a half — clearly identifying and analyzing the top executives who were to be the audience for this event.

What we needed to know was each person's:

- Background
- Corporate rank
- Relationship with sales
- Personal as well as managerial interests
- Personality and temperament

We talked these things over with our presenters, wrote down the findings on large pieces of paper, and tacked them to the walls where they could be seen by all as we developed our strategies.

The managers involved in the meeting were:

- Group vice president of sales
- Vice president of sales
- Vice president of marketing
- Director of advertising
- Regional sales managers

Group discussion produced the following information that profiled the key players:

Group vice president of sales. He was respected by the reps for his intelligence and was liked for his genial personality. He was also new to the company and to the industry — having recently moved from another, quite different consumer products company — and therefore was not fully aware of corporate history or culture, or the specific problems of the business. Because of this, he was something of an unknown quantity. Also, although he carried the highest title, his function in the meeting was not one of direct authority or responsibility. In essence, his concerns reflected those of his immediate subordinate, the next man on the list.

Vice president of sales. He was the executive head of the sales department, the sales reps' bosses' boss. This was really his meeting. He was well known to the reps and, though demanding, was thought to be reasonable, fair, and competent.

Vice president of marketing. He was considered by the reps to some extent an adversary for two reasons. First, there had been tension between the marketing and sales departments for some time, marketing contending that sales wasn't doing a good enough job pushing the product line, sales maintaining that they needed better products with lower prices. Second, he was by nature a challenging and nit-picking person, more numbers than people-oriented, aka the "Sam Donaldson" of the group.

Director of advertising. He was pleased with the sales force. Once his ad campaign was launched, the reps really went out and hustled the products that were advertised, making him look good. Further, the company did a lot of cooperative advertising (that is, it shared the cost of ad campaigns run by retailers who sold the company's products), so the sales team was a vital link in the overall advertising strategy. He was basically an ally.

Regional sales managers. These were the immediate bosses of the sales-people with whom we were working. They were, of course, 100 percent behind the reps, since they worked together closely. But the culture of this particular company dictated that in these semiannual review sessions the reps were on their own; sales managers were not expected to intervene on their behalf. For that reason, they were not likely to make much substantive contribution to the proceedings.

Using this detailed audience profile as a foundation, we went on to consider content and the structuring of the six individual presentations that would be given by selected sales reps. Each of these contained a primary selling point, and within the group of presentations we were careful to include several WIIFM messages, carefully tailored to speak to the interests of each of the principal audience members.

In particular, having identified the vice president of marketing as a potential trouble source, we were able to reduce his antagonism by:

- Anticipating many of the issues he might raise and preparing to respond to them
- Addressing his interests within the messages
- Understanding that resolving the ongoing tension between marketing and sales was not the responsibility of the salespeople, but of the respective vice presidents (in other words, no matter how tough this guy was, the reps weren't working for him; it was their boss, the vice president of sales, that they had to satisfy)
- After clearly identifying the personality type, anticipating expected behavior and taking it in stride

CASE STUDY 2: This example shows the value of premeetings with key players. In fact, some presentations are just a formality since all the key players have already had a one-on-one look at the information.

Our client was a manager at a pharmaceutical company and was representing a study group that had been given the task by senior management of making recommendations on whether the company should enter another line of business. She would be presenting the group's findings to the corporate management committee, which consisted of the president and CEO, the CFO, and vice presidents for marketing, finance, legal, licensing, corporate human resources, planning, and research.

The group's bottom line message was that the company should enter this line of business, and they were proposing three possible means: Outright purchase of an existing company, internal development of a new company with products and sales force, or developing a line of business by co-marketing with an existing company.

Knowing that she would be presenting to very important corporate executives, our client knew she needed to do a very thorough audience profile. Each of these officers had his or her own business priorities.

Here are the significant findings:

- The vice president of marketing, having established the study group, was the pivotal power person — the main person who needed to be satisfied that the study group's findings were valid.
- The vice president of finance had a reputation for asking tricky questions about numbers.
- There was some ongoing tension between the presenter and the vice president of licensing, who had previously confronted her with some rather testy questions in similar circumstances.

This audience profile suggested to our client that in addition to including WIIFM messages for all the principle players, she had better lay down a representation foundation:

- As a courtesy (since he was the spark plug of the project) and to make sure there were no surprises, she made a preliminary presentation to the vice president of marketing.
- She did the same with the vice president of finance, since she hadn't done a complete financial analysis. This eliminated the possibility of embarrassing numbers questions in the full presentation and effectively made an ally of a potentially dangerous opponent.
- She approached the vice president of research, who agreed to deal with the difficult questions the presenter anticipated from the vice president of licensing.

With the help of these preliminary maneuvers, the presentation went quite well. The group's recommendation was only partially adopted, but its work won general approval.

THE PERSONAL TOUCH

Before we leave the audience profile, there's one more aspect of audience identification you should give some thought to — Personalization.

The more often you can make reference to concrete aspects of your listeners' lives — names, places, events, situations — the more you create in them a feeling that you share these things, that you are "one of them." This subtle change in your status — you're not just a speaker, you're a community member on some level — diminishes the barrier of separateness that naturally exists between strangers, so you are heard more clearly.

This may mean doing research or simply putting to use information you may already have. Whatever the effort involved, personalization adds a valuable dimension to your presentation.

If, for example, you're in Springfield to talk about developments in microcomputer marketing, instead of talking about retailers in the abstract, why not use Mike's Megabyte Computer Store down the block, a company many of your listeners may do business with, as an example in your discussion.

If you're a senior at Carnegie Mellon University, interviewing for a job at Anheuser Busch, you will naturally do enough research to sound as if you're familiar with the company. Why not go the extra yard and find out something about Purina and some of the other large companies headquartered in St. Louis, not to mention the city itself. You want to sound as if you are familiar with the company's community and using this information in your presentation will help you make points effectively.

If your presentation opens with a futuristic fantasy about a homeward-bound commuter calling on his wrist-radio telephone to tell his preprogrammed oven to start dinner, why not set the stage on the "Five fifty-seven out of Penn Station," or whatever train your listeners have been taking home from the office most of their working lives? Touches like these create a picture your listeners can easily step into.

This personalization technique works for internal audiences as well. Opening lines might be: "Gary asked for an update on Delta project" or "Following Beth's overview of marketing plans, I was asked to isolate the twenty-one- to forty-year-old segment." The personal touch draws others in, makes it *us*, not just *you*.

To add the personal touch you need to think about the people in your audience. Do you share a common experience with them? Maybe an affiliation, a career path, a boss? Perhaps it's worth the time to visit the manufacturing plant, the sales office, the downtown area. The little bits of information you pick up in this way, the little touches you add, can make all the difference.

QUICK REFERENCE SUMMARY

- Effective presenters are both speaker- and audience-centered.
- Satisfying the WIIFM (What's In It For Me?) syndrome of your audience is crucial.
- Know your audience — their agenda, personal biases, level of knowledge on subject, level of interest.
- What is your message to the audience?
- What do they need or want to learn?
- Create a bond by using common threads that run through the group.
- Analyze your relationship to the people you're presenting to, such as boss, peers, or community members.
- Be aware of special circumstances: press conferences, awards, etc.
- Who are the particular people in your audience who need to be persuaded?
- What are their habits (such as consistently late arrival or challenging attitude)?
- What are their attitudes toward the issues?
- Who will oppose and support your position?
- What are the "hot button" points — issues on which you can expect controversy?
- Know the answers to likely questions.
- Try to foresee problems and work them out before the presentation.
- Use what you know about your audience to personalize your presentation. If necessary, do a little research into your listeners' lives.

When, Where, What . . . and Why: Times, Places, and Things

"To every thing there is a season; a time to every purpose under heaven" (Ecclesiastes 3:1). This includes presentations.

* * * * * *

If you ever have the choice, the best time to schedule an important presentation is Tuesday morning at ten or eleven o'clock. This isn't really based upon scientific research, but it makes sense.

* * * * * *

Why? The key to the answer is attention. Tuesday mornings are the point in the five-day-work-week cycle when people's minds are least likely to be occupied with other matters. Wednesdays around the same time are a good second choice. Third choice is mid-afternoon between two-thirty and four o'clock on either of these days.

Earlier or later in the week, people are preoccupied with the weekend, past or approaching. Early in the work morning, their minds are occupied with the transition from home to work: the rigors of the commute, the mail, and starting the daily schedule. After eleven-thirty or so, lunch begins to loom large. After lunch, the digestion process literally takes oxygen away from the brain and concentration suffers. If lunch involves drinks, concentration may be shot for the rest of the day. If not, there is a period in the middle of the afternoon when people can focus clearly on business — before the mind turns to going home.

These are not cynical observations, but facts about human beings; facts that you need to take into consideration when planning your presentation.

IF YOU CAN'T PLAN, ADJUST

Very often we don't have control over the time of a presentation. In fact, with the growth of telephone and videoconferencing, you may be presenting to colleagues who are literally twelve hours ahead or behind you in the day. So why raise the issue? While you may not be able to pick your time, you can anticipate the quality of attention you are likely to encounter from your audience and structure your presentation accordingly.

For example, if you find yourself appearing at the Breakfast Club on Monday morning or addressing the sales force at four-thirty on Friday afternoon just before they're about to leave to catch a plane to Boca Raton for the semiannual sales conference, you can adjust your approach and maximize the possibility of getting something useful across.

Most often, this means simplifying; zeroing in on one or two checked points and making them as forcefully and as frequently as you can in the time available.

There are other factors that affect listener attention and should be taken into consideration in your presentation planning.

Meals. Sometimes your presentation may take place in conjunction with a meal. In this situation, you will be competing with the digestive process, which favors the stomach over the brain. People are usually fairly alert first thing in the morning, even after a good breakfast. But following a lunch or dinner, your audience is likely to be at least 25 percent asleep. (If alcohol has been served — something you should always try to find out beforehand — it may be more like 75 percent.)

> **TIP:** If your audience is sleepy, one of your few chances to wake them up is to try to get them to stand up or move around a little. You might come prepared with some simple survey question: "How many of you have two or more television sets in your home? Please stand up, so we can see you. Now, how many of you standing have more than two? Just raise your hands. Thank you."

Numbers. Another circumstance that arises frequently is being one of a number of speakers or presenters. At many companies, for example, the budget review process involves meeting after meeting, presentation after presentation, a marathon of facts and figures.

Knowing where you fit into *the parade* can help guide your preparation. If you know you're the fifth presenter — meaning that you will begin long after people's normal attention span is exhausted — you can at least try to compensate.

When you are scheduled to present after the audience's attention has dissipated, your choices are to use an especially striking opening to rekindle their attention (see discussion of "grabbers," p. 47) and/or to hone your presentation to its bare essentials, concentrating exclusively on key messages.

SITE SURVEY

To plan effectively, you need to know the physical location of your presentation. If you don't know what to expect, you're likely to be in for some surprises, and surprises of this kind are almost always unpleasant.

Find out:

- Room size
- Layout and seating
- Lighting
- Equipment

Information about presentation site is likely to be of most concern to those giving public presentations in unfamiliar locations. If most of your presentations take place in your living room, the community center conference room, or the company boardroom, you'll already be familiar with the basic setup. But taking things for granted is taking unnecessary risks. We suggest that you use our checklist and eliminate all uncertainty, whatever the location.

PRESENTATION SITE CHECKLIST

Space, Layout, and Seating

- How big is the room? (Smaller rooms are more conducive to audience participation.)

- What is the seating arrangement?
  — Conference table
  — Chevron
  — Auditorium
- How visible will you be when not speaking? Will you be "on stage" for the whole proceeding, or will you enter and exit? Is there a room where you can warm up? Will your image be projected on a screen?
- How are the sight lines? Will you be able to see everyone? Will they be able to see you? Will you be blocking anyone's view of the screen when you show visuals?
- What does the speaker's platform or area look like from the audience's viewpoint?
- What is the visual background? Can you alter it (draw a curtain, for example) or dress to harmonize with it?
- Is there a lectern? How tall is it? If you stand behind it how much of you will the audience be able to see?

Lighting and Temperature Control
- Is the lighting at the speaker's platform adequate for you to see your notes?
- Will you be able to adjust this lighting?
- Is the room lighting variable (as opposed to on/off)?
- If you need to show slides, will the room be so dark that you will be invisible?
- Will you be able to adjust room lighting without leaving your speaking position?
- Will you need to turn on air-conditioning or adjust the room temperature since lights, equipment, and a certain number of human bodies tend to raise the room temperature?

Audiovisual and Sound Equipment
- Does the room contain the audiovisual equipment you need?
- Do the projectors, if needed, actually work? How about backups? Are spare bulbs nearby?
- How and on what are projectors positioned? Are they handy to the lectern? Are they easy to move?
- Will you need amplification? If so, what kind of microphone is available? (Your best choice would be a wireless mic or, if that's not available, a clip-on. These restrict your physical mobility much less than a fixed lectern or "goose neck" mic.)

- If refreshments are to be served:
  — Is the necessary equipment available?
  — Are you responsible for ordering food and setting up? Is there adequate space?
  — Are there enough electrical outlets to plug in the coffee urn and whatever audiovisual equipment you plan to use?

IF IT'S WORTH DOING . . .

The attention to equipment and other physical arrangements can take a good deal of time, but it needs to be done well. If these elements aren't completely invisible to the audience, they're getting in the way of your message. If the event is very important, you may find it worthwhile to follow the example of theatrical directors and hold a technical rehearsal, in which every aspect of lighting, sound amplification, and visuals presentation is run through *exactly as it will be* in your *actual* presentation — whether by you or an assistant. This means actually using the microphone you will be using (and if it is a clip-on, practicing putting it on quickly and properly; see p. 173). It means actually projecting your slides to verify that the projector is working, that you or your assistant know how to operate it smoothly, and that your slides are properly set up. It means setting lighting and sound levels and making sure these are easily replicated by marking the necessary controls and switches. You should be able to run through all the necessary checks in ten minutes or so.

Whether or not you decide to run a full tech rehearsal, checking and using the physical setup well before presentation time pays a huge dividend in peace of mind. It eliminates potential surprises, and ensures that, mechanically at any rate, things will go as smoothly as possible. This will leave you free to do what you're there to do — make your point.

> **TIP:** *To ease the process of setting up and checking out the presentation site, it's a good idea to approach the person in charge of the premises directly. In a public facility this would be the manager or custodian. For the boardroom, it might well be the CEO's assistant. Whatever the case, the person with responsibility for room scheduling and accommodations can be invaluable in helping you make sure things are properly set up.*

QUICK REFERENCE SUMMARY

- Best time to make an important presentation: ten to eleven a.m. Tuesday. You're more likely to have listeners' *attention*.
- If you're in the middle of a group of presenters, find a way to make your presentation stand out.
- If you can't control the circumstances, you may have to adjust your goals and *simplify* your message.
- Check presentation site for size, seating, audiovisual facilities, lighting, and temperature control.
- Rehearse at the site *with the equipment*. Use the sound system, make all the lighting changes, run the projectors.

Building Strong Messages: Selling Points, Sound Bites, and Word Power

It is now time to be speaker-centered — time to consider your message and how to express it in the most powerful way possible.

* * * * * *

Strong messages use vivid, unambiguous language. They rest on a foundation of information presented in a package that we call a selling point — or in media terms, a sound bite — which makes a positive statement and then gives proof with an example or illustration.

* * * * * *

BACKGROUND: SOME THOUGHTS ON SELLING

The word *selling* may strike you as odd or inappropriate in this context. So, before we turn our attention to selling points and persuasive language and their roles in building strong messages, we'd like to take a moment to clarify our thinking in this area.

As we see it, nineteen times out of twenty, when making a presentation you're really there to sell. Not necessarily a product or a service; it might be an image or idea, a course of action, a point of view — even yourself.

When we ask our workshop clients what their presentation or communications goals are, we get a pretty standard array of answers. The list generally includes: to educate or inform, to solve problems, to arrive at decisions, to agree on a course of action, to persuade, and, yes, to sell.

You'll notice that most of these — all but the first, really — have a clearly active component. We want people to *do something,* based on what we are saying. We want our listeners to agree with us, to approve the recommendations we are making, to make the decision we are supporting. We want readers, viewers, and listeners to actively pay attention and then go out and buy products, or support a cause or a candidate.

Those of you who have some experience in sales understand not only the obvious — that a sale is persuasion — but also that a sale is agreement; that a sale is arriving at a decision; that, very often, a sale *is* the solution to a problem.

And even those of you who present to inform or educate might consider for a moment whether there isn't a more active purpose to your presentations than simply to impart information. You probably also want your listeners to *do something.*

Suppose that you are giving a presentation about cardiopulmonary resuscitation. Aren't you there to do more than simply inform your listeners of the existence of this life-saving technique? Certainly you're there to give them some insight into how it works, but more importantly you want to convince your listeners to *learn* CPR so they can save lives. In essence, you want active listeners.

Many of us are uncomfortable with the idea of selling. We feel that selling "isn't nice." Perhaps this comes from our experience with certain types of salespeople. Who knows? But the reality is that our society is built on selling; it goes on *all the time* in our culture. Calvin Coolidge put it this way: "The business of America is business." And that means selling.

Our point here is not that you should become a slick, fast-talking, hard-sell artist; rather that conscious awareness of your underlying goal can provide *focus* to your presentations. And a focused message is a strong message. The more conscious you are of an *active* goal, the more powerfully your message will be communicated. You want your listeners to do something; you want, in effect, to close the sale.

RETENTION FACTORS

In addition to making your point powerfully, focus contributes to retention. You want people to remember your message long enough to act on it. Unfortunately, this is not so easy to accomplish. Here's one key fact for you to remember about communications.

✳ ✳ ✳ ✳ ✳ ✳

People don't remember much.

✳ ✳ ✳ ✳ ✳ ✳

As we mentioned in Chapter 1, the classic research of psychologist Hermann Ebbinghaus tells us that half an hour after a presentation, the average listener has forgotten 40 percent of what was said. By the end of the day, 60 percent. By the end of a week, 90 percent will have been forgotten. The significance of this cannot be overstated.

If you really want to make your point — if you want it to be remembered — you had better make it *clear,* you had better make it simple, and you had better make it, as an anonymous wit once put it, "the way they used to vote in the Windy City — *early* and *often.*"

Clarity, simplicity, and *repetition* — the words a successful presenter lives by. A message that is not clearly and emphatically stated will quickly be forgotten. A complicated message — or too many messages — may not be absorbed by listeners. A message presented once — as the conclusion of a closely reasoned argument — may not even be recognized as a message!

SELLING POINTS

Creating selling points is a particular way of crafting information into an instrument of persuasion. We've already asserted that it is the foundation of a strong message, but what *is* a selling point?

> **Example:** It's very rewarding being part of the Jaycees; we're a people organization. Seeing Mary Foster win the wheelchair sprint at the Millbrook Special Olympics was worth all the time I've put in over the years.

Notice that this selling point consists of two elements: a positive statement or assertion (the Jaycees is a rewarding organization to be involved with), which we call a *headline,* and an illustration that backs up or proves the assertion (this experience was worth all the time given), which we call a *specific.* A headline can be any positive statement about your company, service, product, program, project, or research. The specific can take many forms: statistics, examples, anecdotes, third-party proof, visualizations, and analogies, to name a few.

Both components — headline and specific — are necessary. Without the specifics, you can't justify the headline. Without the headline to act as a pointer, the significance of the facts may be overlooked. When you use these elements together, your message becomes focused.

Most people just give the general statement — such as, "Our company is a reliable, high-quality service organization." They fail to go the extra step and provide a specific — "Did you know that the city government just hired us to maintain all of Springfield's police and fire alarms?" — that *demonstrates* the validity of the headline. It's the specific, not the headline, that actually gets most of the attention. And the more a specific can capture a listener's attention, the better it makes your point.

CASE STUDY 1: We were asked to assist a spokesperson for Campbell's Soup prepare for a news media interview with a national publication. The article was to be a "round-up" story; the reporter was planning to interview product managers from several companies for an article on a specific item — Frozen Food Microwaveable Dinners. We knew that to win in this interview, the spokesperson would need a few memorable, pithy examples that backed up his general views about the business and his product.

Our first question to the spokesperson: What will you tell the reporter when he calls? The response: "Campbell's Soup believes in quality and freshness." Knowing the company, we knew this to be true, but also told the spokesperson that this statement was too bland and was not quotable.

"Here's an example," said the spokesperson. "In our Chicken Oriental Le Menu product, customers at focus groups told us that the water chestnuts were getting soggy. You see, the dinners go along on an assembly line and we had a machine that would drop the chestnuts on the dinners as they went along. Now, at no extra charge to the consumer, we have a person who hand places the water chestnuts on the dinners as they go along."

"Eureka," we said. We told the spokesperson that he had now created a selling point, or in media terms, a "sound bite" — a headline, backed up with specific facts and information. When the reporter called, the spokesperson began the interview: "At Campbell Soup we are committed to quality and freshness. Let me give you an example of something we have done as a result of focus group research. . . . ." What finally made the article? The details about the water chestnuts. Why? Because they were visible and memorable.

CASE STUDY 2: The research director for a large corporation was making his presentation at the annual budget review. To justify his budget allocation, he needed to allay general management's concern that research wasn't contributing materially to the corporation. His contention was that although the department would never be a profit center in itself, it contributed to virtually every other division.

His *headline*: "Research is important." His *specific*: "One of our researchers developed a substitute for a high-priced ingredient in a food product that saved the brand over *nine million dollars* per year."

Differentiation: The above are examples of statements that stand out, that *differentiate* your comments from others in a presentation, media interview, speech or job interview. In a world of message-clutter, it's critical to develop the ability to create messages that survive the clutter, i.e., are memorable.

Empowering Language: Put a Tiger in Your Talk

The strongest selling points are the ones that appeal to people's "gee whiz" or "I didn't know that" response — and/or hit them in one of three other vital areas: the heart, the tummy, or the pocketbook. The more vividly they do this, the more likely your listeners are to remember your messages. Perhaps not the actual words, but at least the point.

Our primary tool as presenters is the spoken word. But there's another important tool that's often overlooked: our listeners' imagination. If we can use our speaking to engage the audience's imagination, we can get our messages across powerfully. If people can visualize your point they become active listeners. The key to powerful language in presentations is really quite simple. Don't tell, *illustrate*.

This approach is especially effective when applied to statistics or numbers. Though we use numbers a lot as communications tools, they can be quirky. Since Western science describes the world and its events primarily in numerical terms, as a culture we have a very high regard for numbers, almost a reverence. We equate numbers with *facts*. On a personal level, we're able to reject numbers as abstractions and tune them out.

❋ ❋ ❋ ❋ ❋ ❋

If you have a statistic that you feel makes your point, find a vivid way of illustrating it and you will multiply its impact several times over.

❋ ❋ ❋ ❋ ❋ ❋

CASE STUDY: The American Lung Association had come up with a very powerful number that they were trying to impress on the public: Every day nearly one thousand people in this country die prematurely of smoking-related diseases. That's disturbing, but it's just a number; easy for most people to tune out. "Almost a thousand people a day" isn't enough to really get the average person's attention, so we helped them explore alternate ways of presenting the same information.

Almost a thousand people a day adds up over time; it's equivalent to about 360,000 people a year. That has a bit more impact; it's harder to mentally exclude yourself from a group that size. But it's still just a number. To give it power we needed to relate it to something, to make it concrete.

"That's like Giants Stadium filled five times over" was one idea we came up with. Not bad, but it had two problems. First, for anyone who doesn't know how big Giants Stadium is, it doesn't mean much. Second, it fails to underscore the main idea: death on a large scale.

Finally we came up with a presentation that would hit home to just about everybody: "Almost one thousand people in this country die each day from smoking-related illnesses. Imagine it. That's as if two fully loaded jumbo jets collided over your hometown every day — and everyone aboard was killed. We would do something about the air traffic problem that was responsible. Likewise, we should do something about the smoking problem."

You can almost see that scene of the planes crashing and the wreckage and carnage on the ground. This is a painful image, but it is the type of image the ALA wants people to have — to *actively* see in their minds' eyes, and perhaps be motivated to take action.

What was the impact of this selling point? When delivered in the US Congress it made the Senators and Representatives sit up and take notice. Of all the messages delivered by numerous witnesses, this was the "sound bite" that was used on the evening news. And the analogy was so impressive that former US Surgeon General C. Everett Koop used it for several years in his own presentations.

Selling Point File

Creating good selling points doesn't require a consummate literary gift, but it does take thought, attention, and imagination. We suggest that you keep an active selling point file — especially if you present to "external" audiences. In external presentations your listeners often have little or no real stake in you or your message; there is no common task orientation, as there is in a business meeting. This means your messages have to be stronger to make your point.

Good headline material — points you might need to communicate comes up all the time. Write these points down in a notebook or on file cards along with whatever statistical evidence substantiates them. Don't ignore newspapers and magazines as potential sources of material.

Then spend some time creating supporting illustrations, analogies, or visualizations that really bring them to life. Don't go too far; some analogies work, others stretch the imagination beyond the point of receptivity. If you do your work conscientiously, you may come up with several compelling specifics for any given headline. This gives you the option of remaking the same point in a fresh way.

This approach works for "internal" presentations, as well. For example: "The new personnel policies and regular staff meetings have improved productivity. George Smith says that lateness is down 15 percent. More importantly, George told me that Felix Jones is working harder and said he felt like he had more of a stake in the organization."

Keep adding points and working with the ones already in your file. You can't have too many selling points. The opportunity to deliver a selling point can come up at any time in a presentation. The better yours are worked out, the more impact they will have. And the more you practice the art of creating selling points, the easier it gets.

WELL-CHOSEN WORDS

Communicating clearly is not an easy matter, even when all parties have the best intentions. Words can convey meaning with intricate precision, but they have an equal capacity to mislead. Carefully chosen words are more likely to carry the meaning you intend than carelessly chosen ones. Here are our two principles of presentation language.

* * * * * *

Use simple, everyday language as much as possible.
Use strong, active, and, above all, positive words.

* * * * * *

Keep It Simple

In general, try to use one word, preferably a short one, where several might do. If you must use technical jargon or industry buzzwords, define your terms.

It would be foolish to let your vocabulary make your point unintelligible. If your message hangs on one or two key terms and those terms aren't understood, then your message is wasted. Assuming that your listeners share your special vocabulary is a pitfall — you can't be sure.

Acronyms are particularly problematic because they are ambiguous. "OTC," for example, may mean "Over The Counter" to both a stock-broker and a pharmaceutical manufacturer, but to a travel agent it means "one stop charter." In the telephone business it means "operating telephone company," which is also known as a "LEC" (local exchange company) or a "BOC" (Bell operating company). Compound that ambiguity by the number of acronyms we encounter every day and the potential for misunderstanding is astonishing.

For clear communications, don't use esoteric, trendy, or highly technical words and terms — especially acronyms. If you're absolutely sure that the people you're talking to speak the same private language, go ahead and use them. But can you be sure?

> **CASE STUDY:** We once gave a session with people from two different telephone companies, both of which sold an alarm monitoring service. The companies marketed the same product under different names — one called it "Scan Alert," the other "React." We discovered during the session that people from each company were unaware of the trade name of the other company's product.

The point of this illustration is not that you must avoid using a trade name in your talk. When you do use a trade name or any other term that listeners *might* be unfamiliar with, add a brief explanation (e.g., "Scan Alert — that's our alarm monitoring service . . ."). It's simple to do, and it can make the difference between the success or failure of your presentation.

Make It Strong and Positive

There is another dimension of message building we want to cover here. Modesty, which many of us are taught as a cultural value in childhood, dictates that we refrain from "blowing our own horns." As a consequence we often refer in neutral terms to accomplishments that we are proud of. Modesty, however, is out of place in selling.

We want you to look at each of your selling points and notice your wording. Can you find a word that says it more positively? More emphatically? This means using affirmative terms like "I believe," "I know," or "I recommend" instead of the relatively neutral terms "I think" or "It seems."

For example, if your company has to meet federal standards in doing business with the government, this may be a fact you mention in your presentations as an indication of product quality. But compare these statements: "We meet federal standards in this area" and "We *exceed* federal standards." The latter statement sends a much more powerful message.

Instead of a colorless statement like "I think this proposal should be approved . . ." — assuming you truly believe it — an emphatic phrase like "The research really convinces me . . ." leaves listeners no doubts about exactly where you stand.

Signal Words, Themes, and Triplets

There are three more specific ideas we'd like to cover before we leave the topic of words.

Signal words. As a presenter you want your listener's undivided attention, and you may come close to that goal at times. Realistically, you should realize that people's attention does wander, but that it can be summoned back when it's especially important for you to have it. You have to send out a signal that says, "Pay attention!"

Signal words like "What's significant here," "I want to stress," "Let me underscore," "What's important here," or "This *can't* be overemphasized" send that kind of a message. Review or summation phrases like "In conclusion," "To summarize," or "Let's review" do the same. These words put the audience's attention back where it should be — on the speaker. Most of us remember the ultimate signal words, "This will be on the test." We all paid attention.

Themes. As you create the powerful images that give life to your messages, look for a phrase that might serve as a theme, a special idea or image that sums up your message. An image like this can be woven through your talk, building power and retention through repetition and remaining in the listener's memory long after the rest of your message has disappeared.

> **CASE STUDY:** Benjamin Lambert, chairman and CEO of Eastdil Realty, Inc., a major real estate investment organization, was preparing for an

industry conference talk in San Francisco when he came up with the image of the amber light.

The traffic light analogy is an investment business cliché. Investors and brokers are always talking about investment red lights and green lights. One of Ben's fundamental points, however, was that in the real estate market, the light is almost never either green or red. In real estate, one is virtually always proceeding on the amber light of caution.

We liked the analogy and suggested that he make it his lead, work it into the body of the speech, and use it again as a close. We even helped create a little anecdote for the opener about the country's first traffic light, erected in Cleveland in 1914. And so was born the Amber Light Theory of real estate investment. The image got such a strong response that within a week the idea had made it from one coast to the other, by word of mouth. A potential client in New York, who had not attended the session, later told one of Lambert's executives that he had heard the theory — and agreed with it.

Think about this point for a minute. Imagine if you could come up with a compelling story, example, or analogy that someone in your audience would remember a week or two later. This would clearly indicate that you were a better, more effective communicator.

Triplets. Experienced speakers, writers, broadcasters, and others whose livelihoods depend on effective use of language have long been aware that three words are often better than one. (Please allow us this exception to the "one word where several will do" advice, above.)

There's something mystically powerful about grouping words in triplets. It's one of the oldest tricks in the book of rhetoric and memorable examples abound, especially in oratory and advertising: "blood, sweat, and tears . . ."; "government of the people, by the people, and for the people . . ."; "round, firm, and fully packed"; "snap, crackle, and pop . . ."

Learn to think in threes. It can add punch to your selling points and your key messages.

QUICK REFERENCE SUMMARY

- Think of your presentation as if you were selling; it will help you focus your message.
- Your message should ask your listeners to do something: to vote, to decide, to act.
- Clarity, simplicity, and repetition aid retention.
- Selling points are the foundation of a persuasive presentation — whether or not you are literally selling.
- A selling point consists of a positive statement — a *headline* — backed up by a supporting illustration or *specific proof.*
- Look for vivid, visual ways of illustrating your selling points — images that make your listeners see your point.
- Use simple, everyday words; avoid technical jargon and acronyms.
- If you must use technical language, jargon, or industry buzzwords, explain them.
- Use strong, active, positive words, not guarded or negative ones.
- Use signal words and phrases to keep the audience tuned in: "The real issue is . . ."; "What's important here . . ."; "This is critical . . ."
- Look for visual themes that can tie a presentation together.
- Use words in groups of three to increase audience interest and retention.

The Three-Minute Presentation Writing Technique

Somebody once asked Abraham Lincoln how long it took him to prepare a speech. "It takes me about two weeks to write a good twenty-minute speech," he said, "but I can write a forty-minute speech in one week. And," he added, "I can give a two-hour talk on almost any subject right now." Or, as a correspondent of ours once put it: "If I'd had more time, I'd have written you a shorter letter."

The point? It's hard to be concise.

With our three-minute presentation writing technique, however, we give you a way to cut the job down to size. Once you are proficient with it, you should be able to draft your presentation in three minutes or less, regardless of length. Our technique works whether you make thirty-second, five-minute, or two-hour presentations.

Not only is it fast, our writing technique also gives you an important psychological edge. Think of the times you've sat down to write a presentation, a memo, or a report and gotten stuck trying to come up with a lead. Remember the days before word processors, how those crumpled pages piled up on the floor? Our method relieves you of all the frustration of getting started because the lead will come later.

The technique centers on two easy steps:

1. Stating your conclusion
2. Listing your arguments

[Note: For those who want a slightly different approach — but one that also focuses on stating your conclusion and listing arguments — see Chapter 6 on Mind Mapping.]

43

These elements comprise the core of your presentation. Almost the entire structure flows from them. A third element is often necessary to complete the scheme, and that has to do with the "lead" we just mentioned. We'll discuss that later.

The first step is the key, but it rests on doing something that does not come naturally to most people. The natural tendency in formal communications seems to be to save the conclusion — the recommendation, action plan, sales pitch — for the end. Our writing technique, however, reverses that process.

STEP ONE

Make a succinct, one-, two-, or three-line statement of your message; the bottom line of your presentation.

By the time you're ready to start writing you should be able to do this fairly easily. If you can't, the chances are you're not ready to write.

This point of departure acts like a mental funnel, channeling your whole thought process into a tightly focused output. It makes for a stronger presentation because it forces you to focus on your *message* rather than your argument.

    ❋ ❋ ❋ ❋ ❋ ❋

In communications, arguments are secondary. The first priority is to make clear what is being proposed; then the supporting facts can be introduced to bolster the conclusion.

                                   ❋ ❋ ❋ ❋ ❋ ❋

CASE STUDY: A client of ours, a research scientist with a pharmaceutical firm, provides an excellent illustration of why this is so important. She came to us to improve her presentation skills following her first experience in presenting to senior business management.

True to the scientific method in which background and data precede the conclusion, our scientist launched into an hour's worth of data related to her projects. After about three minutes, the president of the company slammed his hand on the conference table and demanded, "Do we have a new drug here, or *don't we?*"

For him, this was the bottom line. If the answer was yes, then he wanted to hear the details; if it was no, the details were irrelevant. If it was maybe, he could decide, but without knowing the point of the message, a lengthy exposition was unacceptable.

The principle illustrated by this example is true even when it's not a go/no-go situation, as in the preceding case study. Look at it from a listener's point of view: When you know where an argument is leading, you can judge how well the points substantiate the conclusion as the argument unfolds.

In a sense, the facts that make up the argument are just packaging; they usually won't be remembered.

Another thing to consider is that in many informal presentation situations (in the hall, in the elevator) you may be cut off at any moment. Even in formal meetings you never know what key figure may have to leave early. So, whatever the circumstance, give them your message early.

Where to Start

Begin. Grab a pad and a pencil; you're ready to start creating your presentation. First state your conclusion, your recommendation, and your action plan. Most often this should take the form of a direct call for action.

You'd be surprised how many presenters never really tell their audience what they want from them. This is true even of salespeople: According to Hank Trisler, author of *No Bull Selling,* 63 percent of sales calls end without the salesperson ever asking for the order. We want you to formulate your message so that you make it absolutely clear what it is you want them to do. Here are a few examples:

- "Lease a car from us. It will give you convenience, flexibility, and reliability."
- "I recommend that we reorganize our materials supply system and keep this plant open."
- "Volunteer some of your time to the United Way; you'll feel better about yourself and our community will be stronger."
- "My committee's recommendation is that the management invest 4.7 million dollars in this new line of business. We'd like your approval."

What's *your* conclusion? Write it down. Say it out loud. How does it sound to you? Make it clear and strong. You're off and running. Once your conclusion is set, the rest of your presentation should fall into place.

STEP TWO

List the selling points that support your conclusion.

These elements — your *conclusion* and *action plan* and your list of selling points — form the backbone of your presentation. Here's how it works:

Conceptually, we divide presentations into three sections:

- Beginning
- Middle
- End

    in which you:

- Tell 'em what you're gonna tell 'em
- Tell 'em
- Tell 'em what you told 'em

The beginning and ending essentially mirror each other, stating your conclusion and briefly summarizing the supporting material. The middle, the body of the presentation, consists of discussing that material in detail.

Let's look at the specific structure of each segment.

Beginnings

The function of your opening is to clearly state your message, to outline the argument that supports it, and to prepare listeners for the detailed discussion that will follow. It has another function as well. In addition to introducing your message, your opening is your big chance to really get your listeners listening.

Perhaps you know the story about the old farmer who came upon a neighbor one day, trying to get his mule to go. The man was shouting and cursing and pulling on the bridle — all to no avail. Picking up a handy piece of two-by-four, the farmer whacked the mule between the ears with all his might. The mule shook its head. The farmer shouted, "Gee-up!" The mule blinked for a moment and then started forward. "The problem is," explained the farmer, "you first got to get his attention."

Think of the attention span of today's Zippers and Zappers, aka Channel Surfers. (Zippers are those who fast forward through the commercials on programs they have taped on videocassette recorders. Zappers or Channel Surfers change TV stations with their remote controls.) Few listeners or viewers give a station much time before flicking the dial. It's often a matter of seconds. But the producers of programs and commercials don't want us to fast-forward or change the channel or station. In the presentation arena, you have a little more time — about 30 seconds before people tune you out. If they don't leave the room, they think about errands they have to run, the weather, work piling up on their desk, the movies. If we admit to being Zippers and Zappers, then you can see why it's important to have a strong opening or grabber in a presentation.

❋ ❋ ❋ ❋ ❋ ❋

Attention is a prerequisite to communication. The more of the audience's attention you have, the more communicating you can do.

❋ ❋ ❋ ❋ ❋

Here is the third element in the three-minute presentation writing technique, relating to the "lead."

STEP THREE

An introduction that captures your listeners' attention is a necessity.

It doesn't matter *when* this element gets created. Despite the fact that it will be used in your introduction, it can be the last step in your preparation.

The Grabber. Since audiences can be quite mule-like, a presenter needs a verbal equivalent of the two-by-four in our story. You want not merely to capture your listeners' attention but to really engage their minds. We call this kind of attention-getting kickoff the *grabber*.

The appropriate degree of "grab" will vary from one type of occasion to another. Generally, your grabber doesn't have to make the stars fall from the sky or shake the pillars of the temple. It should introduce the topic in a catchy, arresting, or amusing manner, or it should introduce you, creating a connection between you and your listeners. If it can do both, even better.

We use three types of grabbers:

- The anecdote
- The prop
- The bottom line

At its very simplest, your grabber can be something as transparent as relating a pertinent thought, insight, or observation that "occurred to me as I was driving out here this morning." Or perhaps, "I was talking to Amy just before the meeting, and she was telling me some of her concerns about test market results on the product." Personal references like these help break down barriers between you and the audience by establishing a connection, even if it's a small one. Perhaps the easiest grabber is to look in the daily newspaper just before your presentation. You can almost always find a news story that relates to your audience and the topic: "You may have seen today's article in the *Wall Street Journal* on . . . That relates to my topic. . . ." The audience has either already read the article, or now knows what to do after the presentation, or at the very least, gets a mental image of the *Journal* masthead and will pay more attention to you.

The Anecdote. Humor is good bonding material, which makes it a valuable ingredient in openings. We don't, however, recommend jokes as grabbers, because even seasoned pros like David Letterman fall on their faces about 30 percent of the time. Also, it is difficult these days to tell most jokes without running the risk of offending someone in your audience. But almost any anecdote such as a personal story with a laugh — or just a smile or "ah-ha" — can do the job. Good material of this sort is often close at hand.

> Case Study: A woman in one of our workshops had compiled a comprehensive report on what in the telecommunications business is called "corridor traffic" (that is, phone calls between major markets that cross state lines, say from Camden, New Jersey, to Philadelphia). Her presentation about the report was interesting and informative, but it lacked a distinctive opening.
>
> In a casual conversation with us, she mentioned that she had become a minor celebrity around the office as a result of her efforts. Her colleagues had dubbed her the "corridor queen." We pointed out that this would make a terrific opener: "Let me tell you how I came to be called the corridor queen . . ." She'd had it in her head all the time; it just hadn't seemed relevant to a public presentation.

Personal, whimsical touches like these pull an audience in. You wouldn't necessarily use this type of grabber for the chairman of the board, but it would work fine for a group of peers.

Even an amusing play on words can make a good grabber.

CASE STUDY: A new vice president of marketing at a midwestern phone company who was new to the telephone business was convinced an acronym describing Local Access Transport Areas (LATAs) would never be understood by the public. She wanted it changed.

The company's advertising director, however, had studies that indicated that LATA had gained a high recognition factor within the industry and that changing the terminology at this point would be extremely costly. Her message was, "Let's keep things the way they are"; and status quo can be a lot harder to sell than innovation. She wasn't going to astound anyone with what she had to say, so in keeping with her low-key message, she came up with an effective grabber: "Good morning. We're here today to discuss the LATA matta'. I believe that LATA is here to stay, and in support of this I'm going to give you some LATA data. . . ." — which she then proceeded to do. And recognizing a good thing, she mirrored the opening in her conclusion: "I hope that now we'll be able to lay the LATA matta' to rest."

The Prop. There are times when you'll really wish you had a two-by-four for an attention-getter. We really don't recommend this, but sometimes the right prop will do the job.

CASE STUDY: A product manager we know was once the fourth of six scheduled presenters at a morning sales meeting held in Montevideo, Uruguay. To begin with, a lot of salespeople don't want to be bothered with information. Their attitude is, "All I need to know is what's the price and what's my cut." And in this particular setting, their minds were mainly on the sightseeing they would be doing as soon as this meeting was over.

His topic was the chemical properties of the company's new shrink wrap — a subject the salespeople would need to know when they talked to customers. How to get their attention? This was his solution:

"You will notice that I have placed on your desks two oranges. One is shrink-wrapped, the other is not. I want you to take these home and put them on your kitchen windowsill. Call me in a month and tell me how they're holding up. I guarantee that the orange that isn't wrapped will be a shriveled wreck. The one that is wrapped will look just about the way it does now.

"Then take a knife and cut into the shrink-wrapped orange. You'll find it as fresh and sweet as any orange you could buy at the store that morning. Now. Let's talk about the chemical properties of this improved shrink-wrapping."

The Prop helped to penetrate; it got a "gee whiz" response by graphically and dramatically illustrating something significant about the product. The presenter still had to go through his overheads, but the Prop and explanation were interesting enough to hold their attention for the time he needed to make his point.

The Bottom Line. Whether it's combined with a prop or anecdote, almost every presentation should have a clear statement of your bottom line.

The stunt with the oranges is really a dramatization of a selling point. Very often a strong selling point makes an excellent grabber. Especially effective selling points are those that stimulate the intellect, provoke our "gee whiz" response, appeal to our sense of self-interest or well-being, or touch one of our emotional buttons — hitting us in the heart, the tummy, or the pocketbook.

CASE STUDY 1: Probably one of the toughest audiences any presenter could face, in terms of attention-getting, are the passengers on the New York-Washington, D.C., air shuttle. These people are busy and stressed. They've heard the air safety instructions scores of times.

Knowing this, the stewardess on one recent flight began her spiel with the following: "Did you know that flying is the safest form of transportation? Safer than riding a bicycle or a train?" With this grabber, she caught the attention of the normally blasé passengers.

She continued with her Bottom Line/Action Message: "But safety is everybody's responsibility, so please take out the card from the seat pocket in front of you and read along as I review the information. . . ."

Our rough estimate was that about one-half of the passengers did indeed reach for their instruction cards and seemed to be following along — about a tenfold increase over a normal shuttle flight.

CASE STUDY 2: A client of ours was involved in marketing an order processing software package. In her presentation, she mentioned one implementation in which this system had reduced 350 days of order processing time to 5 working days. We suggested she make this her grabber: "If we could help you boil down an entire year's order processing work into *one week,* wouldn't you be interested in learning something about our services?" This bottom line selling point was so strong we encouraged her to use it in her closing as well.

We could go on about grabbers, but we've certainly given you some ideas to work with. Whatever opening gambit you hit upon, it should lead directly and naturally into the statement of your bottom line (if your grabber does not, in fact, contain your message), after which you can briefly outline the body of your talk. And that's your beginning.

* * * * * *

Once you have worked out the beginning of your presentation, we strongly recommend that you commit it to memory.

* * * * * *

During the first moments of your interaction with the audience, you want to be able to mobilize all your communications skills, which means making eye contact with your listeners and having your hands and arms free to gesture (see Chapter 9 for a detailed discussion of delivery skills). Memorizing your opening lets you concentrate fully on your delivery.

A final thought on openings and grabbers: Although you may think we're pushing you to become vaudeville performers with all this razzle-dazzle, we really just want you to be strong presenters. We actually welcome the opportunity to tell presenters to tone it down. If you have doubts about any of this, think for yourself how you respond to presenters who drone on and on, or take a long time to come to the point. We feel strongly that it's better to *challenge* your listeners than to leave them to their daydreams.

Middles
The middle of your presentation is the guts. It's where the information is imparted and the persuasion takes place. It may contain:

- Supporting data
- Statistics
- Evidence
- Research
- Findings
- Proof

Without good, hard information in the middle, all the audience profiling and message tailoring in the world isn't going to mean much. Paradoxically, this information is the part of your talk people are most likely to forget, but it is still a vital element. It is the material the audience needs to make decisions. If it's not there — or it's not convincing — you are *not* going to succeed in making your point.

Likewise, a ho-hum approach to the structure and the wording of the middle of your presentation can cost you the whole ball game. Strong visual imagery in your selling points, colorful or surprising illustrations and examples, and well-planned visuals can all add sparkle to the middle of your talk. They will help sustain interest and attention, but they are no substitute for solid facts.

Don't fall into the trap of putting all your time and effort into the Ending and Beginning and leaving the middle to take care of itself. If the body of your talk is boring or ponderous, it will completely undermine even the strongest opening. And it doesn't matter how stirring your closing is if you've already lost your audience.

There are four basic ways to structure the middle of a presentation. We call them:

- Question and Answer (Q & A)
- Problem/Solution
- Time/Sequence or Timeline
- Topical

Question and Answer. The Q & A approach analyzes a problem or task and puts it into a series of questions that need answers. For example, "The questions we need to explore in our marketing plan are: What type of media support do we have? What are our sales objectives? and, Where does the sales force tie in?" After setting this agenda, the presenter then covers the individual questions and answers in detail.

Problem/Solution. This scenario works well for reporting results and generally goes something like this: "As you know, we've been facing a serious and unanticipated cash-flow problem, stemming ultimately from a troublesome deterioration in accounts receivable. We were asked to study the situation and develop some measures to correct it. We found that both the average age of receivables and percentage of overdue accounts had risen sharply in the first quarter. We also found that our reporting system made it extremely cumbersome to track down the specific information that would help us take appropriate action . . ."

In other words, the Problem/Solution scenario involves a concise statement detailing the elements of the problem, followed by an outline of how solutions were developed, leading into a detailed discussion of the significant stages and findings. This kind of a middle would naturally culminate in an emphatic selling point something like: "With our new reporting system up and running we have been able to reduce the average age of receivables from sixty-one to forty-seven days, which is far below industry standards. And we're happy to report that cash flow is looking better than it has for years."

Time/Sequence or Timeline, This approach stresses the history or chronology of a process, problem, or issue.

CASE STUDY: Marc Chodorow, a former vice president of public relations for Goldome Bank, a national banking company, used the timeline approach when he was representing Goldome to the press or to securities analysts. A thumbnail version goes roughly like this:

"Between December 1981 and March 1982, the former Buffalo Savings Bank, whose assets were 3 billion dollars, acquired three troubled thrift institutions. Assets grew to 9 billion dollars. In early 1983, the organization became Goldome (named after the gold-domed building that had been the institution's home since 1901). The year 1983 also saw the creation of our mortgage banking company and insurance agency, and the acquisition of two savings and loans in Florida. In 1983–84, we created a merchant banking group. In 1985–86, the new corporate headquarters were completed in Buffalo, incorporating the original building and thus symbolizing the progress from a regulated savings bank to a diversified national banking concern. In 1986, we recorded our highest profits ever, and in 1987, Goldome went public."

Another Time/Sequence example would be the pharmaceutical product manager explaining to new management recruits the process of getting a new product to market; running down the sequence of events from preclinical testing through application for FDA approval, product design, tooling up, clinical testing, packaging design, advertising and promotion development, to actually getting the drug to the sales force and into hospital formularies and onto pharmacy shelves.

Topical. This method is probably the most common. Basically, it says, "Here are the topics that need to be dealt with or resolved in situation X." As with all these approaches, it is important that you provide your listeners with a good road map. For example, you might begin, "There are several topics we need to explore in evaluating this acquisition. . . ." But instead of proceeding to exploring them one by one, take the time to list them first: "The topics include the Dependable Company's product line, the cost and payment terms of the acquisition, and the synergies between our two companies." Then go through the list. This way, each topic is like fitting a brick into place; listeners anticipate the structure of the argument and watch it take shape.

✹ ✹ ✹ ✹ ✹ ✹

If there are many facts in the middle of your presentation, it is a good idea to summarize your progress from time to time.

✹ ✹ ✹ ✹ ✹ ✹

It's like erecting signposts for your listeners. "Now that we've covered the issues of cost and product lines, let's discuss the topic of synergies . . ." If you've given a good clear opening statement of your objective you can reinforce that objective as you move through your points by explicitly referring back to it. For example, "Keep in mind that these numbers and statistics help prove the overall soundness of the marketing plan and should be considered when you vote later on . . ."

Endings
You've told 'em what you're gonna tell 'em and you've told 'em. Now it simply remains to tell 'em what you told 'em — and to drive it home.

Briefly summarize the points of your argument and restate your message. To get the maximum impact from your restatement, you need to introduce or set off the ending with a signal phrase like "Let me summarize what I've said . . ." or "In conclusion . . ." "Flagging" your conclusion increases its impact by focusing your listeners' attention; it alerts them to the fact that you are about to tell 'em what you told 'em. If they weren't paying close attention before, they will respond to this signal and pay attention.

The whole ending should rarely take more than a minute.

✷ ✷ ✷ ✷ ✷

Like the opening, your ending should be memorized.

✷ ✷ ✷ ✷ ✷ ✷

The reasoning here is the same as for the beginning: The end of your talk is the last thing your audience will hear, and the last thing heard is the thing most likely to be remembered. The more clearly and forcefully it is stated, the greater the likelihood that it will be remembered accurately. Memorizing your ending lets you concentrate on clear and emphatic delivery, with your eyes looking up at people in your audience.

RECAP

Here's our three-minute presentation writing technique in a nutshell:

1. Write your conclusion or bottom line.
2. List the supporting material — your selling points: data, facts, statistics, research, examples.
3. Find an appropriate grabber.

Once you're familiar with the process you can go through it quite quickly — three minutes or less — when you need to. The technique works whether you're sitting in your office using a dictaphone, or in an airplane seat using pencil and paper.

In fact, the technique can be condensed into the "down and dirty thirty-second writing technique." And there are people who can use this. Pharmaceutical sales reps come to mind. They catch a doctor coming out of the elevator or the hospital cafeteria and very often they have literally thirty seconds to make a pitch. Something like "Hey, Doctor Smith, I know you're just out of surgery and you haven't slept in four days and you have to go on rounds, but let me tell you the four reasons why our new drug is a better preoperative sedative. . . ."

Even if you don't normally work under these conditions, you may find the thirty-second technique comes in handy once in a while. You never can tell when you're going to find yourself in the elevator with the president of the company — that never-to-be-repeated opportunity to let the boss know — in person — what you've done for the organization lately.

QUICK REFERENCE SUMMARY

The three-minute presentation writing technique begins with two primary steps:

1. Write your conclusions, including an action plan.
2. List your supporting arguments (selling points).

These elements form the core of your presentation: beginning, middle, and end.

- Writing the conclusion first helps clarify and focus your thoughts.
- It is vital to gain an audience's attention within thirty seconds of beginning. Think "What's in it for them?"
- Develop a grabber to pull in the audience. Grabbers are pertinent thoughts, insights, observations, analogies, personal experiences.
- Avoid jokes; they fall flat too often.
- Props dramatize points.
- After the grabber, the beginning of the presentation will mirror the ending. The key point goes *up front.*
- The middle of a presentation contains hard evidence; data, statistics, research.
- Presentation of the middle is vital to your credibility; take the time to do it well.
- Visual imagery of selling points, colorful or surprising information, and well-planned visuals add sparkle to the middle of a presentation.
- Presentation middle can be designed in one of four ways:
    1. Q & A — asking and answering vital questions on issue.
    2. Problem/Solution — posing problems; offering solutions.
    3. Time/Sequence or Timeline — chronological orders of events to make your point.
    4. Topical — listing topics one by one, addressing them individually.
- Ending contains two elements: summary of key points and call for action. Tell audience what you want them to do.
- Set off your ending with signal words, summarize your arguments, and leave them with your action plan ringing in their ears.

CHAPTER **6**

Mind Mapping

The three-minute presentation writing technique discussed in Chapter 5 falls into what we'll call the *traditional* method for organizing a presentation. It is similar to the outline method of taking notes. The techniques are fairly linear, although we break from total orthodoxy by recommending that you start with your conclusion and make sure you support your argument with persuasive information.

An alternative method for organizing a presentation is decidedly non-linear. It still requires you to focus on the bottom line information and supporting arguments, but it allows for more brainstorming and creative thought before you finally order the presentation.

We call the technique Mind Mapping. It's also known as cluster thinking, brain web, and left-brain thinking. These nonlinear modes of thinking encourage creativity, because they combine the use of words and symbols, color and format, integrating the strengths of both brain hemispheres. Creativity is one of today's communications and business buzzwords. Everybody wants it, companies and their supervisors are looking for it. Mind Mapping can be your path to presentation development and note taking when you're listening to presentations.

* * * * * *

Nonlinear methods of thinking encourage creativity by integrating the use of both brain hemispheres and capitalizing on all their strengths.

* * * * * *

RIGHT HEMISPHERE, LEFT HEMISPHERE

The brain is divided into two halves, the right and left hemispheres. Each half has its own strengths. The right hemisphere concentrates on artistic, creative traits: rhythm, color, movement. The left hemisphere focuses on logical, analytical subjects like numbers, letters and formats.

Traditional note-taking and presentation methods like outlining appeal primarily to the left hemisphere. They rely on strict formats, a set progression of numbers and letters. Mind Mapping, however, allows for a freer flow of ideas to the paper. Putting the ideas down is more important than where they are placed on the paper or what order they occur in. Mind Mapping, through a combination of form and function with visual ideas and relationships, integrates the strengths of both brain halves, increasing efficiency and creativity.

Mind Mapping allows your mind to brainstorm along many different paths at once. It does not force you to proceed in a logical manner, to produce ideas about one subject at a time, in a specific order. Instead, Mind Mapping encourages all your ideas.

❈ ❈ ❈ ❈ ❈ ❈

You should be sure to write down even those seemingly unrelated points that pop into your head while brainstorming.

❈ ❈ ❈ ❈ ❈ ❈

One of Mind Mapping's strengths is that it allows you to look at all your ideas in new ways, with new connections and associations. *This is creativity.*

Mind Mapping allows your mind to empty itself onto paper. It is important to let this process happen uncensored. Allow yourself to put down everything that comes to your mind, even if it seems totally unrelated. Follow thought trails through to their end — a relationship you didn't see at the beginning could become apparent.

While judgement is important, don't try to apply it too early, or you run the risk of shutting out valuable new lines of thought and their related ideas and associations. When you begin to think about a subject or focus, let your thoughts wander and flow. You want to be able to see every possible association, connection, and pattern. Editing can come later.

Do not censor your ideas while Mind Mapping. Write down anything that occurs to you. You may see a relationship later in the process.

MIND MAPPING: THE PROCESS

While there is a form and a method to Mind Mapping, there is no strict set of rules. The process is yours to individualize, to customize so that it works best for you. You may even use it in different ways for each project.

The elements of Mind Mapping include a central focus or core idea, which is placed in the center of the page; and uncensored ideas, key words and phrases to represent ideas. Each key idea is connected to the central focus with lines, *color is used to highlight* and emphasize ideas; *images and symbols are used to highlight* ideas and stimulate the mind to make other connections.

Mind Mapping is simple; there is no wrong way to do it. All you need to begin is a blank piece of paper, something to write with, and an idea.

When you are through, your Mind Map will present a visual answer to your problem, question, or situation. You will be able to look at it, both throughout the process and when you think you are done, and see new connections between your ideas, new ways to relate your points to each other. Here is a blueprint of a basic Mind Map:

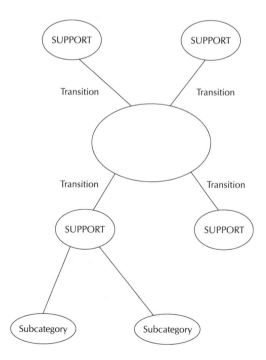

The circle in the center is the hub, the central theme, the bottom line of your Mind Map. The circles connected by the spokes will be sub-themes — or depending on how your map turns out, ideas that end up in a wastebasket before doing a presentation.

To begin the Mind Mapping process, decide on your main idea. Your Mind Map will grow very differently from your research, knowledge of the different ideas, even if they seem similar. Once you have decided on your central idea, you are ready to start drawing.

Perhaps it will be easiest to understand Mind Mapping with a hypothetical example. Let's say you are scheduled to make a presentation to the local Kiwanis Club on the service project for the upcoming year. You have concluded after substantial thought and research that the project should be to rebuild a local park damaged by a fire and vandalism.

The first thing for the Mind Map will be to write down your main idea, or a picture to represent it, in the middle of the page, and draw a circle around it. This is the core idea of your map, from which idea branches and new associations will grow. Now, write down the ideas that come to you, connecting each with a line to the main idea. It is critical to use only key words or phrases because you want to capture your thoughts quickly — just enough information to stimulate your memory when you go back later to review.

For example, some of the other supporting circles might include key ideas such as:

- Benefits for the organization
- How the project will be organized
- Budget
- Competing ideas not selected
- Hurdles to complete the project
- Impact on the community

Each of the sub-themes should have its own smaller circles or bubbles or supporting information. If you don't have any support (aka proof) for the sub-themes, it's not a subject worth bringing up in your presentation. But it's important to at least put the idea down on the map.

After you complete all the brainstorming, it's now time to think about how to organize the information. Much of the organization depends on your audience. For example, if it's a presentation to the budget subcommittee, you might start with the budget bubble and then go to the bottom line of the project. If it's a project where the individual talents of your members will be well used, you might start with an anecdote about John Doe and his work with Project Habitat and lead from that to the core idea of the local project.

The Mind Map is also helpful for handling questions and bridging to your core ideas or sub-themes. (See Chapter 10 for Bridging.) You might get a difficult question about liability insurance for building the park. You should answer the question, but may also be able to return to the main idea for the project and perhaps bridge to other ideas.

A sample Mind Map on writing this book might look something like this:

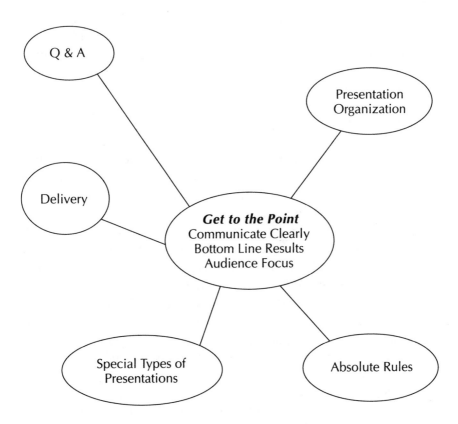

The core idea of this book is to be user friendly and help people who have to organize and deliver presentations. Since our primary focus is learning how to *Get to the Point* and be direct, that makes sense to be the core message, or center of the map. The other sub-themes should now be obvious from either a look at the Table of Contents or reading the book. Each of the sub-themes or bubbles is supported by details and information.

We could go through all the bubbles, but let's leave that for the individual chapters.

HOW TO USE MIND MAPPING

Mind Mapping has many applications other than presentation preparation. Use it anywhere you need to be creative and efficient: writing a report, article or book; organizing a project; brainstorming for solutions to a problem; creating an agenda for a meeting; note taking in a meeting; sorting out your ideas on a subject for your own personal growth.

At the Presentation

Your Mind Map can be a wonderful guide at your presentation. For the three-minute presentation writing technique, we recommend note cards and bullet points. If you use a Mind Map, you can literally bring the one-page map as your set of notes. You may have other supporting material, but this is your guide.

We particularly like Mind Maps for presentations to boards of directors or other groups where you anticipate frequent interruptions for Q & A. With a highly organized presentation, you may get thrown off by a question or two. With the Mind Map, the question merely represents one of your sub-themes or bubbles. If the question comes from a subject that's not covered on your map, either you've not been thorough enough in your preparation, or more often, you can table the discussion of that topic because it's not germane to *this* presentation.

Mind Mapping and Media Interviews

We believe that most media interviews are a type of presentation, where you have an opportunity to communicate your points. (See Chapter 16 for a full discussion of media interviews.) Once you have figured out why the reporter wants to talk with you, and you know the angle of the story, you can put the map together with a core idea and supporting information. The connecting bubbles can represent your support, difficult questions, and what your competition or opponents might say. When answering questions and bridging, the Mind Map gives a spokesperson a "home base" or central theme to return to, and a path on another spoke to a new subject.

QUICK REFERENCE SUMMARY

- Nonlinear thinking increases efficiency and encourages creativity by incorporating both halves of the brain.
- There is no wrong way to Mind Map.
- Don't censor your ideas; relationships may appear later.
- Use color and pictures to highlight important ideas.
- Stick to single words or short phrases to describe an idea.
- Use Mind Maps for interactive, Q & A-intensive presentations.
- Mind Maps work well for print media interviews.

Noteworthy Notes

You may or may not want to write out your entire presentation as you develop it, but you'll almost certainly want to have some sort of written material with you as you deliver your talk.

We feel very strongly that a presenter should use notes, rather than a full transcript. It is much harder to achieve the spontaneous conversational tone that is appropriate to presentations when reading from a full transcript. You almost inevitably sound like you're "giving a speech," which feels wrong to the audience in most presentation situations. Notes support the conversational mode, prompting and reminding you of what you want to say.

The most frequent question we get is, "How extensive should my notes be? What do I put down and what do I leave out?" Actually, the two questions, "how much" and "what," are not the same.

How much? Clearly, we can't give you a specific answer to this. It's going to depend on such factors as how long your presentation is, whether you give it once or often, and how much factual or numerical detail it contains. But we can offer a general answer — which is, "Probably a lot less than you think."

* * * * * *

Notes should be a reminder, not a transcript.

* * * * * *

Especially when people are new to presenting, they will begin by writing out a talk fully and then whittling it down to a few sparse notes. Others prefer to start with a detailed outline and pare that down. It may take a few presentations to get an accurate feel for what is important to have in front of you and what isn't.

* * * * * *

Less is more. The more material that goes into your notes, the harder it will be for you to extract what you need.

* * * * * *

The art of note making lies in achieving a balance between completeness and accessibility. As you include more information in your notes, either the word density increases to the point where your eye has trouble finding what it's looking for or you end up with too many pieces of paper.

What to write. Start with the idea that your notes should at least reflect the organization of your talk. This means at a minimum they should clearly list, in order, the points or topics you wish to cover. This will make sure you don't leave out anything you planned to say. Or, if time gets short, it lets you *choose* what to skip over and what to include.

You can use "bullets" (heavy black dots) to list your points or, if you prefer, number them. Numbering will be especially helpful if you open with a remark like, "There are really only four things that this committee needs to know about enzyme detergent additives."

Stay away from complete sentences. Generally, a word or two or a short phrase, will be sufficient to suggest each point you wish to cover.

* * * * * *

In general, list facts and anecdotes, not principles.

* * * * * *

Under stress, we tend to forget "facts" — specific anecdotes, references, numbers, examples. The facts listed on note cards will always lead us to the larger point, but it does not work the other way. If their accuracy is crucial, the details in your notes should be things like exact numbers or statistics, and lengthy quotations. Other things included will be cues for particular stories or anecdotes, cues for visuals, and personal reminders.

TIP: *Some experienced presenters dispense with notes altogether by working the information that would otherwise be on note cards into their visuals. This is a good idea un-*

less it pushes you to include more visuals than taste and reason would otherwise dictate. Further, if your equipment malfunctions, you can be up a creek. Play it safe and have a hard copy of any notes you'll really need.

How to write. Print clearly, preferably in block capitals. Or type your notes. Keep notes sparse; leave as much blank space as is practicable to maximize legibility. You've probably all seen presenters who made their notes too small or wrote too much and had to squint to make out the key words. We don't want this to be you.

⊛ ⊛ ⊛ ⊛ ⊛ ⊛

Make sure your notes are readable.

⊛ ⊛ ⊛ ⊛ ⊛ ⊛

TIP: *You can use colored pens or highlighters to make crucial facts or cues virtually jump off the page. Red is the most visible for writing or underlining, but other colors work well, too. In fact, you can "code" your notes by using more than one color: for example, red for reminders, blue for statistics, green for quotations, and orange for anecdotes. Yellow isn't very readable, so you won't want to write with it; on the other hand, it is excellent for highlighting (marking over words to make them stand out).*

Another possibility is using colored index cards to code the different sections or areas of your presentation. One color each for beginning, middle, and end. A colored card for your facts and figures. A colored card for your final summary points. The possibilities are limited only by your needs and ingenuity.

What to write on. You can make notes on virtually anything. Legend has it that Abraham Lincoln wrote the Gettysburg Address on the back of an envelope. If that's all you have available, fine; but other things work better.

* * * * * *

Five-by-seven-inch file cards make the best note cards.

* * * * * *

File cards are best because the heavy paper stock stands up to normal wear and tear. We recommend the five-by-seven size because, in our experience, that is the best compromise between legibility and manageability (smaller and you either have to write small or you can't get much on one card; larger and they become awkward to handle — and conspicuous). They are best used in the vertical or "Portrait" orientation, perpendicular to the way the lines are printed, so you will want to use the blank side. Writing across the short dimension of the card helps keep notes short and concise.

> **TIP:** *If you plan to follow your talk with a Q & A session, make a separate card listing important selling points you made during your talk, points important enough to be repeated.*
> *Glance over the card before you begin your Q & A, and refer to it from time to time as you field questions. You can also jot down on this card any vital numbers, facts, or statistics you need to have at your fingertips for answering questions.*

CASE STUDY: Here's a concrete example of how a set of presentation notes might look. Six sparsely worded five-by-seven note cards were all Andy needed for a forty-minute presentation to an audience of eighty lawyers in a course designed to improve their courtroom skills and techniques.

The message of the presentation was that *how* a lawyer communicates can be as important as what he or she says. The talk referred primarily to opening and closing arguments during a trial, but was also applicable to questioning of witnesses before a judge or jury. Andy's action message was to ask the lawyers to be aware of this aspect of trial work and to practice the techniques he would demonstrate to improve their skills.

The stated assumption in the talk was that there was no substitute for a good case with good witnesses and the facts and/or the law on your side. But all things being equal, it is very often the better presenter or communicator who convinces a judge or a jury.

But the question here is: What did Andy put on the cards?

```
                                                    Note Card 1
  1. AG
     CCI

  2. NOTICE ME
     SUIT
     LIMP
     TIE

     TENN.
     IDAHO
     FDA
```

Andy's first remarks concerned his name and a brief statement about CommCore and our business.

Next, Andy asked people what they noticed about him as he walked to the front of the room. The points, in case he didn't get much response, were that these lawyers, or members of a jury (their audience) would notice a suit, the fact that Andy was limping due to a recent injury, and maybe that he had a red "power" tie on.

The third set of points were grabber points (see our discussion of "grabbers,") to convince the lawyers that judges and jury members still wanted to be entertained. The notes were Andy's cues for short anecdotes about events in Tennessee, Idaho, and the Food and Drug Administration. These anecdotes all led to the conclusion that judges, commissioners, and other decision makers are supposed to base their judgments on the facts a presenter gives, not how it is presented. These anecdotes also let Andy's audience know that these decision makers are also human beings influenced by how things are communicated. What's important about his notes is that he wrote down the anecdotal note, not the conclusion. From the anecdote, he could always get to the conclusion. However, if he'd just written a note about the conclusion, he might have forgotten to mention Tennessee or one of the other examples.

Andy concluded his opening with a statement about the purpose of the talk.

```
  3. — Ct. Room Scenes                             Note Card 2
       Inherit the Wind
       Pat & Mike
       Perry Mason

       The Verdict
       LA Law
       (Imperfect)
```

```
┌─────────────────────────────────────────────────────┐
│   4. — CONTRAGATE                                     │
│      Brendan Sullivan                                 │
│      John Niels                                       │
│      Arthur Liman                                     │
└─────────────────────────────────────────────────────┘
```

Andy next asked the lawyers to name some of their favorite court-room scenes. This was part of an attempt to make the talk interactive. His note card list of movies and TV shows was in case the lawyers didn't come up with suggestions, or in case he wanted to bridge to a point.

The "(Imperfect)" point was to remind the lawyers that part of their comments related to impression, but they should not be thrown off by the "perfect" world of the tube or the silver screen. The courtroom is a more "imperfect," real-world environment.

Point four related to several comments Andy wanted to make about the Iran/Contragate congressional hearings, which were then going on. His comments were more about the lawyers involved than the key witnesses.

```
┌─────────────────────────────────────────────────────┐
│                                        Note Card 3    │
│          IMPRESSION                                   │
│               40                                      │
│               60                                      │
│               90                                      │
│                                                       │
│      7                                                │
│     35                                                │
│     58                                                │
│                                                       │
│     FDA                                               │
│     TENN.                                             │
│     IDAHO                                             │
└─────────────────────────────────────────────────────┘
```

Remember the statistics we've talked about concerning what an audi-ence retains and what makes up the entire impression? Andy quoted them and applied them to courtroom situations, where a jury can al-ways ask for testimony to be read back to them.

"FDA," "TENN.," and "IDAHO" had been on Card 1. However, in case Andy forgot to mention them early on, he wanted to get the points in during the talk. And that illustrates an important point about notes. In some ways, Andy didn't even need the cards. He probably could have used one card with several points. However the cards are a good crutch, as well as a reminder in case he forgot something. During the talk, he referred to them several times. Even at the end of the talk, he bought a moment before his conclusion by saying, "Give me a moment; let me check my notes to make sure I covered everything."

```
┌─────────────────────────────────────────────────────────────────┐
│                                               Note Card 4         │
│                              WIIFM                                │
│      AUDIENCE           Room — set up                             │
│                             charts                                │
│      CONTENT                                                      │
│                                                                   │
│      MEANING —                                                    │
│                   explain                                         │
│            legalese                                               │
│                     Albuquerque                                   │
│            Structure                                              │
│               Shorter sentences                                   │
│               Watch news                                          │
│          Language                                                 │
│              — active                                             │
│        Facts          Analogies          SPs                      │
└─────────────────────────────────────────────────────────────────┘
```

With the note "AUDIENCE," Andy asked the lawyers to be aware of the audience, whether it was a judge or a jury. Clearly, the audience profile would have been done during jury selection. But the point was to be aware of the appropriate WIIFMs (What's In It For Me?). The other point was to be aware of the physical environment and to use the room effectively.

"CONTENT" was Andy's statement that the facts had to be right. However, given facts and content for a statement or questions, the lawyer should be mindful not to use too much legalese with a jury lest they not understand all the information. Andy illustrated this with an anecdote about an Albuquerque lawyer.

"STRUCTURE" cued Andy to mention using shorter sentences in important oral communications and that a good way to learn oral communications skills is to watch good commentators on television.

The "LANGUAGE" notes refer to many of the elements we just covered in the writing chapter. The specific words — "Facts;" "Analogies;" and "SPs" — were points Andy wanted to make.

```
┌─────────────────────────────────────────────────────────────────┐
│                                               Note Card 5         │
│      VOICE                                                        │
│      GESTURES                                                     │
│      EYES                                                         │
│      DRESS                                                        │
│      NERVES                                                       │
│      PAUSES                                                       │
└─────────────────────────────────────────────────────────────────┘
```

As you read further in *Get to the Point* you will learn what we have to say about all these elements. Andy used the cue words to be sure to cover each element and how it relates to communications, impressions, and retention. One word was enough for a one- to two-minute chunk of his talk.

PRACTICE	Note Card 6
EXERCISES	
LISTEN to TV, RADIO	
SMILE	Marion
ENJOY	Seltzer
NERVES	
JACK LALANNE	

These were Andy's final notes about how to apply and use the information in his talk. Each word was a cue. Again, this is much of what we have covered and will cover in *Get to the Point*.

The name on the right was written in at the last minute and was a reference to one of the course instructors Andy met just before he spoke. This was a way to personalize the talk. In fact, he had mentioned Ms. Seltzer earlier in the talk, but the note was here just in case he forgot.

The "JACK LALANNE" note was to remind himself to get the audience members up on their feet and to show them exercises that would loosen them up before a presentation. Everyone present indeed did rise and do the exercises, including a federal and a state judge who were sitting on the dais.

Since doing closing statements and answering questions have long since become second nature to him, Andy made no cards for these parts of the talk. So that's it. Six cards, forty minutes. Try making note cards; they'll work for you, too.

Note choreography. Walking to the lectern or speaker's platform with a handful of papers can add a distracting element to the beginning of your presentation, a transition that you want to go as smoothly and unobtrusively as possible. If you have to put on a microphone, empty hands are necessary. What do you do with your notes? If you use the five-by-seven cards we recommend, they will usually fit neatly in either an inside breast pocket or an outside jacket pocket.

If you like to use large sheets, for whatever reason, solving the problem is trickier. You can fold your notes and put them in a pocket, but this means you will have to carefully unfold the pages before you begin speaking, which can be quite noisy when amplified. Further, once folded, paper has a tendency to fold back up, so unless you go through the cumbersome process of reverse-creasing them, your pages probably won't lie flat and may be difficult to read.

A solution is to leave your notes on the lectern before the proceedings begin. But this creates another hazard: It will be very easy for someone else to inadvertently walk away with them. A covering sheet that says something like "Speaker's Notes — Do Not Remove on Pain of Death" should prevent this. Even safer would be to use the cover sheet and tape the notes to the lectern with removable tape.

If you work without a lectern, you will have to hold your notes. Five-by-seven (or smaller) cards work best in this situation. Lettersize note pages are a distraction — a visual distraction to the audience and a physical distraction to you.

QUICK REFERENCE SUMMARY

- Speak from notes, not from a complete transcript. The talk is in your head; your notes function as a written agenda including vital reminders.
- Five-by-seven file cards held vertically work best for notes.
- Keep notes succinct; a word or two per item.
- Write *facts* or visual ideas on notecards, not general overview statements. Stress reduces the ability to remember specifics. You can always get the statement from the fact, not vice versa.
- Visual aids can serve as notes.
- Use colored pens, highlighters, and cards to help make important information stand out.

Show and Tell:
Visual Communications

Even an accomplished presenter can become better by using visual aids. Visual materials — whether they consist of the latest multimedia computer generated technology, flip charts, overhead transparencies, color slides, films, videotapes, or three-dimensional models or other physical props — can be of tremendous help in making a point. Their skillful and judicious use can add dimensions to your presentation that no amount of extra speaking can contribute.

In this chapter we want to cover general rules for visuals — rules that work no matter what technology you use. Then we'll explore specific rules and ideas for different media and technologies. We'll cover:

- Flip Charts
- Slides
- Overhead Projectors
- Computer Generated Visuals
- Computerized White Boards
- Videofax

● ● ● ● ● ●

A recent study by the University of Minnesota and the 3M Corporation (which updates an earlier study by the Wharton School) finds that an audience is 43 percent more likely to be persuaded by presenters who use visuals.

Another study by at a leading pharmaceutical company suggested that visuals which include pictures or visual images are almost two times more likely to be remembered than the typical words and bullet point visual.

Well designed and choreographed multimedia computer-driven presentations increase your odds even more of having audiences remember and act on the key messages of your presentation.

❋ ❋ ❋ ❋ ❋ ❋

As useful as visuals are, however, we would like to emphasize that they are best used in moderation. Notice that we use the words "visual aids." While we want to enhance our communication by letting our audience see as well as hear, the visual material should be there to assist — *not to control or dominate.*

We make this point because it is easy to get carried away with visuals, to include so many or get so caught up in the technology that they overshadow the main attraction — which is *you.* Visuals are rather like icing: a pleasing complement to cake but cloying if too thickly spread.

You should follow these four rules, explained later in this chapter:

- KISS (Keep It Short and Simple)
- Color
- Coppertone
- Pause

If you do, visuals will add focus to your presentation. But beware: As visuals proliferate, they lose their impact and dull your listeners' attention.

CASE STUDY: In the early days of computer assisted graphics, one company wanted to get a head start on the latest technology, a computer generated graphics device that produces quite professional-looking images, highly detailed and very colorful — images that can grow and evolve right on the screen. A consulting client of ours in that company was among the first to get his hands on this device, and he received many compliments on the fine graphics in his presentations. The problem was that few people could recall the content of his message because it was too cluttered.

The University of Minnesota/3M study put it this way:

"Image-enhanced graphics are effective only when selected and used carefully."

What is the optimum number of visuals to use? We obviously can't give you a specific answer, but we do have a recommendation: Keep them to a minimum. A good rule of thumb is: "When in doubt, leave it out." And for each visual, the rule is: "Less is more."

Limit your visuals to those points that will have more impact visually than verbally and you'll be on safe ground.

* * * * * *

Never begin or end your presentation with a visual unless it is absolutely compelling. Remember, they came to see you, not a media show. For certain presentations where there always is an image on a screen, figure out how to return the screen to a 'neutral' look when it's important for the audience to focus just on you.

* * * * * *

We all sense the truth in the old saying, "A picture is worth a thousand words." But make sure it's the *right* picture in the right place.

The very thing that makes good visuals so powerful is, in a word, *simplicity.*

* * * * * *

A picture that conveys a complete idea or set of relationships in a single visual image is the proverbial thousand-worder.

* * * * * *

One of our all-time favorite ads is the familiar Coppertone billboard, with the little girl and the puppy who's playfully pulling down her swimsuit bottom. It communicates a simple message, uncluttered with extraneous information like the price or the sun-block number. All it really says is "suntan product" — and that's all it needs to say.

* * * * * *

Good visuals work in the same way as a strong verbal selling point — by illustrating, not explaining. And the simplicity and vividness of the imagery add up to high retention.

* * * * * *

Busy and cluttered visuals — complicated charts and graphs, screens full of words — can actually decrease retention. There are two seemingly contradictory reasons for this. First, complex or cluttered graphics present a task — a dense mass of visual fodder for the eye to munch through and digest — that the brain naturally resists. Second, though the brain resists digesting the visual, it will continue to try, and will be distracted from your message. It will return to this annoying challenge and "worry" it. The problem is that, while this is happening, what you are saying will not be heard.

THE BASICS

We have distilled the treatment of visuals down to four basic rules:

- The first, *KISS,* relates to content
- The second, color, relates to execution
- The third, Coppertone, combines content and execution
- The fourth, Pause, relates to delivery

KISS. This is also known as the "Six Pack Rule." When in doubt, simplify; eliminate extraneous material. If necessary, use an additional visual rather than burdening one with more information than it can efficiently transmit.

Different industries define this rule in various imaginative ways, but here are the basics of the "Six Pack Rule": A presentation visual should contain no more than six lines of copy and a "package" or headline on top. The art director of a television news broadcast team put it this way: A visual should contain no more information than what a motorist can absorb from a billboard, driving past at forty miles an hour.

You can bet that billboard ad designers have this down to a science, and they give us thousands of superbly produced examples to study — along the sides of every street and highway. Instead of ignoring billboards, you would do well to give them some attention. They can give you valuable ideas for your own visuals.

Color. Since color movies became standard in the forties and color television — and all its advertising — became the standard in the sixties, we have come to expect the stimulation of color and so have our audiences. The University of Minnesota/3M study confirms that "color is more persuasive than black and white." If possible — and wherever possible — use color in your visuals. In some corporate cultures, it's advisable to use black-and-white overheads. In this environment, judicious use of a red or blue pen to underline, or circle on overheads can add the same dynamic as pre-produced color overheads. We'll go into greater detail as we discuss these types of visuals separately.

Coppertone. The same communications media — movies and TV — have also conditioned us to be more receptive to pictures than to words. If you can, use a picture. Above all, take the time and trouble to design visuals that are as attractive as you can make them. With the advent of computer clip art programs it's very easy to add a visual to most overheads. Your visuals will be judged, unconsciously at least, by the standards of commercial TV production. The legendary Coppertone billboard, with the dog pulling down the swim suit of the little girl, said more about the product that any detailed list of the sun block number or paba content of the product.

The touches you add to breathe life into your visuals can be quite simple; as simple as adding a picture to relieve the severity of type.

> **CASE STUDY:** A telephone company executive was presenting basic information on a service program they were selling called "Linebacker." He had prepared a viewgraph that consisted of a bulleted list of his main selling points, but he enhanced the communications value of this list immeasurably by taking the extra time and trouble to set the words inside the brightly colored outline of a football helmet. This not only gave the audience an image to relate to, it united the selling points in a concrete way with the program's clever name: "Linebacker."

Pause. Whenever you present a new visual . . . pause. If necessary, count, "One hippopotamus, two hippopotamus," to yourself. Here's why: The moment you display a visual, that's where your audience's attention goes. If you are talking while this process is taking place, either you won't be heard or your visual won't be seen. Without the pause, you'll be competing with your own visual.

Many people are afraid to pause, because they're afraid that no communication is going on during the silence. In fact, there is a great deal of communication going on; it's just not spoken communication. Sportscasters Vin Scully and Joe Garagiola won praise and recognition in the broadcasting industry for reintroducing silence in their World Series telecasts. When excitement explodes or tension builds, they let the picture tell the story instead of competing with it.

Do the same when you display a visual. Don't compete with it; give your audience time to absorb it.

A pause of two or three seconds is generally enough if you designed your visual according to our advice. Then you can resume talking.

Say what you have to say about your visual. Then, when you're done, *get rid of it.* Turn off the projector, flip the page, cover the model, put on neutral or logo image, and move in a way that directs the attention back to you. As long as the visual remains on the screen or in view, some or all of your audience will be paying attention to it, not to you. Also, the action involved in getting rid of the visual serves as a demarcation line. It tells the audience, "We're on to the next point."

CHOREOGRAPHING VISUALS

Poorly planned or executed visuals can harm your presentation more than they help. If they are ugly, confusing, or too numerous, they will turn off your audience. By the same token, if they are handled ineptly and if they are not smoothly integrated into the overall performance, they can weaken it more than they strengthen it.

⁂ ⁂ ⁂ ⁂ ⁂ ⁂

The process of dealing with the physical objects involved in presenting visuals can interrupt the flow of the presentation.

⁂ ⁂ ⁂ ⁂ ⁂ ⁂

The cure for this is planning and preparation. During the presentation, have your equipment set up where you intend to use it. Dragging the flip chart or projector to where you are speaking, or making an excursion to the other side of the room to operate your equipment takes too much time. It makes you look and feel hurried and unprepared. If your equipment is set up in advance, when you are ready to use it, the minor pause that will naturally occur as you reach over to turn on the projector or walk over to the flip chart will help "frame" the visual rather than create a major distraction.

> **TIP:** *If you follow another speaker, take the time you need to reset the room for your presentation. A simple statement, "I'll be with you in a moment, I'm just setting up the equipment," will buy you the few moments you need.*

Choreographing the Computer/Laptop Presentation
Computer assisted presentations offer many advantages, but also present distinct challenges for the presenter.

If you're using the computer and a liquid crystal display (LCD), you need to set up room lighting so all images and colors can be seen. Make sure you have a long enough cord for your mouse so that you can click on images.

> **TIP:** *For laptop presentations to more than one or two people, always try to have an external television monitor or liquid crystal display (LCD) with a screen.*

For laptop presentations to small groups, you must know how to display the screen so that all viewers can see the information. Since no two computers are the same, each will have a different sight line for viewing. Laptops also make it difficult for the presenter to be absolutely sure what the audience is seeing. A few models have a side or display screen. If you are not sure what is on the screen at any one time, it makes sense to keep a hard copy of what you're showing.

Mixed media. Mixed media is *not* multimedia. Mixed media refers to the question of: Should I use more than one type of visual aid? Our general answer is that it's better — certainly safer — not to. It just multiplies the possibilities for mistakes and other disasters. It's one more thing you have to prepare in advance, keep under control, and remember how to operate.

That's not an absolute answer, of course. Suppose the sales force is making a presentation to management and everyone agrees to use color slides, but one salesman wants to show the television spot that one of his retail accounts is running. Maybe it's justified, but it will entail turning off the slide projector, adjusting the room lighting, moving the VCR into position, and making sure beforehand that the tape is properly cued up. It can be done and may make a nice change of pace. But unless it is well choreographed and deftly handled, the mechanics may result in slipups and general disruption of the pace of the presentation.

Pointer pointers. If you have things to say about your visual, politeness and practicality dictate that you face the audience as you speak. Many people reach across their bodies to point or actually face away from the audience as they speak, lessening the impact of the visual.

* * * * * *

If you use a pointer, you must hold the pointer in the hand that allows you to both point and face the audience: If your visual is on your left as you face the room, the pointer goes in your left hand; and conversely.

* * * * * *

When you are through using the pointer, it's best to get it out of the audience's view. Set it down or, if it is the telescoping kind, collapse it and return it to your pocket. Having a pointer in your hand can turn the simple act of turning off a projector into a moment of high drama. If you forget to put away the pointer, it becomes a prop. You've probably seen someone absentmindedly brandishing the pointer like a sword, bending it like an iron bar, conducting the *1812 Overture*; generally creating quite a lot of distraction, if not amusement. So, when the pointer has served its purpose, retire it, like the visual, from the scene.

For **Laser Pointers,** here are a few specific rules: Try to avoid pointing to every word; this reminds the audience of "follow the bouncing ball" sing-alongs. Also, try not to point the light at people in the audience — it's quite annoying.

SPECIFIC VISUAL AIDS GUIDELINES

Flip Chart

This is the easiest of the visual aids to use. It is effective for groups of up to twenty-five people or so, and is an excellent way to present simple text or graphs.

* * * * * *

In planning your chart, think in terms of key words, like the bulleted points in your notes.

* * * * * *

Less is more; be terse; use single words or short phrases. Let your commentary amplify the words on the chart. Your audience sees the key word or phrase; you provide the explanation. If you must use complete sentences, or simply prefer it, that's okay. But be consistent; stick to one style. If you use a sentence to start a chart, do the same for all the items on that chart.

* * * * * *

Make your writing as legible and as attractive as you can.

* * * * * *

Unless your calligraphy is above average, it's a good idea to stick with block capitals. Magic marker is probably the best writing tool for this job. Because markers are available in a wide variety of colors, it is an easy matter to introduce color into your charts. Even the simple use of a bright accent to underline helps flip charts come alive.

Writing on a flip chart during a presentation automatically creates a pause, but unless your addition to the chart is quite concise, this pause can be too long.

* * * * * *

The simplest solution to this problem is to prepare your flip charts in advance and flip or tear off sheets as you go.

* * * * * *

Preparing charts in advance, rather than creating them as you present, has the added virtue of letting you do the job beforehand more slowly and carefully.

This idea suggests completely prefabricated flip charts, perhaps produced by the art department. But studies indicate that higher retention occurs if the chart is not actually completed in advance — leaving the presenter to fill in several key blanks, write the last line, or underline key words on the spot. This provides an air of spontaneity, and watching the presenter in the act of creating the visual has special significance for the audience. It is a process; it's an expression of you, not just prepackaged information.

TIP: *While creating your charts beforehand, you can lightly pencil in the words or elements you plan to fill in during the actual presentation. The audience won't be able to see them, but they're good cues for you. Whatever you decide to write on the spot — be it much or little — when you are finished, you still need to stand back and . . . pause. Really give your listeners a moment to take in the finished product.*

Many presenters feel limitations in terms of picture possibilities with flip charts — unless they draw well. Actually, unlike with some of the other kinds of visual aids, audiences tend to be quite forgiving of less-than-professional graphic quality in flip charts. The audience sees you making them and they don't expect you to be a professional calligrapher, designer, or illustrator. We encourage you to think in terms of picture possibilities and not worry too much about living up to a professional graphic's standard.

> **CASE STUDY:** A marketing professor was lecturing students on the concept of "hard goods promotion": the selling of such items as soap powders, cereal, or nails. Rather than simply use written words to enumerate the features and benefits of her product examples, she created a visual with the simple outline of a box of detergent, within which she enumerated the key selling points. This provided a clear, albeit simplified, visual frame of reference for the verbal information.

When you plan to use flip chart visuals, be sure to find out in advance whether anyone else will also be using the chart. If the answer is yes, you will need a way to locate your prefab charts or blank pages quickly. You can easily mark your pages by dog-earring them or by affixing a paper clip. Then, instead of flipping page after page, you can simply leaf through the stack from the side till you find your marker and flip all the pages at once. This not only eliminates a potentially distracting and time-consuming muddle, it will spare you the embarrassment of inadvertently displaying other people's visuals in the middle of your talk.

When you are finished with a particular page, don't leave it there so it can compete with your continuing presentation; tear it off or flip it over.

* * * * * *

Be sure to include blank sheets between your prepared charts so that you can get rid of them — by flipping to the blank.

* * * * * *

Overhead Projector

This familiar device is useful for displaying visuals to groups of up to fifty people or so. The standard overhead, or "viewgraph," projects eight-by-ten-inch transparencies best shown when mounted on cardboard frames. These require some specialized equipment to produce: either a "dedicated" transparency machine or a photocopier that will print on some sort of transparent film. Most of today's "plain paper" copiers will handle this job. (See the box in this chapter on making your own transparencies.)

The overhead projector has been given a new life with the development of laptop presentations that use an "LCD" presentation connection to display computer-programmed visuals onto a screen. (See the section on computer assisted programs.)

Those who don't have direct access to the necessary equipment can use the services of graphics houses or desktop publishing experts, who can handle any stage of the process, from setting type, to artwork, to layout, to transferring a finished layout to transparent film and mounting it on a projection mask.

Like any equipment, the overhead projector requires some prepresentation setup. First, you must be familiar with the equipment you will be using. This doesn't mean knowing how to use an overhead projector; *it means knowing how to use the overhead projector that's there.* Know where the controls are as well as how to operate them. Always make sure during setup that the machine is actually functioning — which will also require you to determine that there is a working electrical outlet where you need it, or the required extension cords.

⁕ ⁕ ⁕ ⁕ ⁕ ⁕

Most important of all, always make sure there is a spare bulb on hand — and that you know how to replace the bulb — or that a working backup projector is available.

⁕ ⁕ ⁕ ⁕ ⁕ ⁕

You don't want to find yourself in the position of one Ph.D. candidate who blew a bulb in the middle of a major presentation of his dissertation and had no backup — whereupon one member of the review committee was heard to murmur, "Now we'll see what he really knows."

To set up, position the machine, turn it on, and focus it, using your first viewgraph as a test. To minimize the muss and fuss of moving it into position during your talk, leave the projector as close to where you will be operating it as you can. (If you can't leave it in the exact position, take a cue from professional stagehands and mark the correct position on the floor with tape.) Assuming no one else will be using the machine before you, you can leave your first transparency on the projection glass, ready to go. Then when the time comes for your first visual, all you have to do is step over to the machine, move it into position if necessary, and flip the switch.

> **TIP:** *If you use viewgraphs a lot, you should consider making a guide to help in positioning slides. Two simple blocks of wood — or in an emergency, even a couple of pencils — fastened to the projection glass in an L configuration with strips of tape should virtually eliminate those awkward moments of looking back over your shoulder, trying to get the image straight and centered. ("Gaffer's tape," used by film makers, or duct tape, available at any hardware store, is the best choice for this.)*

There aren't many rules about the specific treatment of overhead transparencies, but here's one of the most important ones we teach:

* * * * * *

However tempting it may be, avoid beginning or ending your presentation with a viewgraph or slide. It kills the human element.

* * * * * *

As with any visual, remember to *pause* after displaying an overhead; let the audience absorb the information before you begin to talk about it. When you're through discussing the visual, turn the projector off (or change to a neutral logo slide) so the attention of the audience is not divided.

In general, if you have things to say in connection with your graphic, you should step back and talk near the screen, not the projector. This move will insure that audience sight lines are not blocked, and it will encourage you to project your voice a bit more. Remember to face the room and hold your pointer, if used, in the hand next to the screen. If you speak near the projector, there is a tendency to look down at — and thus talk down to — the slide rather than the audience.

If you have a number of graphics to present, especially if they come together in a cluster, try to introduce some variation in your presentation technique to avoid lulling your audience into inattention. You can do this by occasionally introducing the material verbally *before* you present the image. Subtle as it may seem, this is an effective variation on the technique of showing the image and then talking after the pause.

> **Example:** "This next graphic will show anticipated first quarter sales for the new SuperWidget." Turn on projector. Pause. Continue. "You can see in column two, which is outlined in blue, that we expect a 4.7 percent increase over the same period last year." Just remember, whichever order you use for a particular visual, what you don't want to do is present and talk simultaneously.

> **TIP:** *To minimize the number of pieces of paper or props you have to handle, why not put the white cardboard borders of your viewgraph transparencies to work? They make a convenient place for notes relating to your next graphic or your next point.*

One advantage of viewgraphs is that they are relatively easy to return to. This comes in handy at Q & A time. If you *plan* to return to a particular visual or visuals, you can save the trouble of searching by creating duplicates. If you have only a few transparencies you may not feel the need to do this.

MAKING YOUR OWN TRANSPARENCIES

For those of you without an art department or a computer graphics program, but with access to a plain-paper, enlarging/ reducing photocopier, here's our quick and easy home viewgraph production recipe.

Step 1: Type your text neatly according to your layout. Use boldface type whenever possible. You can "paste up" the final arrangement if you choose. (In general, a pasted-up layout gives greater flexibility, but of course it's a bit more work.) Cut out the various elements and carefully position them on a clean sheet of paper. Rubber cement is a standard material for paste-up as it allows for some repositioning and is easy to clean up. Photocopy the finished layout onto a clean sheet (normal size or "100 percent") and white out any hairlines created by the edges of the cut-and-pasted elements.

Step 2: Enlarge your text to the desired size by running it through the enlarging photocopier.

Step 3: Photocopy your completed visual onto transparent film and mount it in a cardboard frame.

Step 4: You now can easily add touches of color by boxing, underlining, or adding exclamation points or other punctuation in brightly colored transparency markers. In fact, if you're willing to use a transparency only once, you can consider adding text or underlining or other colorful touches while you're protecting the visual — just like writing on a flip chart!

One special technique you can use with the viewgraph is to reveal your graphic gradually. (We call this the "striptease effect.") If, for example, you have a list of bulleted points or headlines, you can set up the slide with all but the first one masked off with a large file card or other opaque object. Then, as you get to the next point, move the mask down to expose the next headline, and so on. This adds something of the element of motion and participation that flip charts provide. If you use this technique, remember to remove the mask altogether when you reveal the last element. If you leave the mask there, at least half the audience will be wondering what's still hidden under the file card instead of listening to what you are saying.

Computer Graphics

In the first edition of *Get to the Point,* computer graphics packages were only for the experts. Now, even the novice word processor user can learn how to design passable-to-excellent graphics and visual aids. Graphics can then be made into overheads, slides, hard copy, and/or displayed directly from a computer onto a TV monitor or a screen through an overhead projector with an LCD panel.

Other significant advantages of computer programs:

- Information can be updated at the last minute, even as the presentation unfolds.
- Audiences enjoy bar charts and pie charts that unfold as you present. These charts score well on post-presentation surveys.

- Technology will allow you to connect to a large screen projector and display images for larger audiences.

Like any other aspect of training, *input equals output*. It's easy to learn rudimentary graphics; it takes much more time and a sense of design to put together knock-out visuals. The programs are becoming more user friendly.

❋ ❋ ❋ ❋ ❋ ❋

Avoid the Ransom Note Syndrome.

❋ ❋ ❋ ❋ ❋ ❋

This is the result of people who get so enamored of their programs that they change fonts and type faces without regard for the impact on the viewer. The visual begins to look like the old-fashioned ransom notes which were composed from assorted type faces found in the daily newspaper. The result is that the visual is distracting and the message is not conveyed.

Multimedia

Multimedia refers to the growing capabilities of PCs and CD-ROM devices to allow a presenter to combine graphics, text, sound, and full-motion video on a computer monitor or even a twenty-by-thirty-foot screen.

❋ ❋ ❋ ❋ ❋ ❋

When thought out, designed and choreographed well, multi-media presentations are more engaging for the audience and increase the opportunities for audience retention.
   The video component also allows you to capture a presentation from an expert or co-presenter who can't be with you.

❋ ❋ ❋ ❋ ❋ ❋

As described by Peirce-Phelps, Inc., world's largest integrator of multimedia and videoconferences company, "Tell a group something, and they'll soon forget. Show them the same thing, and they might remember it for a while. But get them involved completely, and they'll respond to your message."

Photographic Color (35 mm) Slides

Color slides are a popular visual medium and are useful for groups of between ten and several hundred people.

It takes careful design and execution to produce top quality slides — the kind of expertise provided by corporate graphics departments or professional third-party vendors. Since slides are more likely to be judged by professional standards than charts or viewgraphs, they have not been the medium of choice for presenters without access to these resources.

Producing professional-looking slides has recently become easier, thanks to developments in microcomputer generated graphics. It's easy now; the art department has been eliminated. Just remember: Easy does not necessarily equal good, and less is often more.

In terms of presentation to your audience, slides are not really very different from viewgraphs, and virtually all of what we have said about the latter applies here (including not beginning or ending your presentation with projected images). There are, however, a couple of comparative advantages and disadvantages to consider.

The main disadvantage of slides is having to darken the room. This creates a disruption in the flow of your overall presentation. Since it tends to be troublesome, there is a tendency to cluster all your visuals together so that you only have to go through this once. This does not necessarily work to the advantage of your presentation.

For best effect, the lighting should be adjusted so that the audience can see you as well as the images. This can be tricky; work it out carefully in advance. Figure out exactly which lights to turn off and mark the switches with tape; or, if there is a dimmer, place a piece of tape next to the dial and mark the correct position so that you or whoever is adjusting the lighting can do it with one motion instead of fumbling around, trying to gauge if you've got it right. This will help minimize the disruption.

TIP: *In halls where slide projection necessitates complicated lighting adjustments, it is a good idea to enlist the aid of an assistant who can handle the lighting and/or the projection duties. The less you have to cope with physically, the more you can concentrate on making your presentation.*

Another minor drawback with slides is that the possibility of physically interacting with the graphics — as in underlining or adding text to a flip chart or viewgraph — is virtually eliminated. You can however, create essentially the same effect as either the revealed graphic or the overlay technique in successive slides. And probably with graphically superior results.

One main advantage for slides is that the sophisticated design of slide projectors makes slides physically simpler to present. It's been reduced to simple button-pushing, which is not to say that it can't be fouled up. As with any projection system, you must always check out the equipment beforehand. While slide projectors are fairly standard, it is essential that you or your assistant know how to operate the projector that is actually there. Make sure the projector is working and that there is a spare bulb or a working backup projector of the same type close at hand.

During setup, check the projector by running through all your slides. Be sure they are in the correct order — and position. You can then leave the projector set up with your first slide ready to go. Fumbles at the slide projector — upside down and reversed images and frantic scrambling to get slides into the right order while the audience stares at the blinding glare of the blank screen — are a classic presentation error. Let it be someone else, not you.

> **TIP:** *If you are changing your own slides, taping the remote control to the side of the podium or lectern allows you to keep both hands free to point or gesture. (Again, gaffer's tape or duct tape is excellent for this.) When you want to bring up the next slide, all you need to do is step over — or lean over — and tap the button. It is also a good idea to put a piece of tape over the backup or reverse button, to spare yourself the muddle and embarrassment of inadvertently showing slides you've already presented.*

Film and Videotape

Although used less frequently than any of the foregoing visual media, film and video work well for certain kinds of presentations. Films can be shown to groups of almost any size. Video is useful for groups up to twenty-five people per monitor. Except for a few details relating to the physical setup, they are essentially the same visual aid.

Our information and precautions for slide presentations (including the desirability of an assistant) are virtually the same for film, adding that you will need to darken the room even more. Know how to operate the projector — which should be carefully set up and tested, including the sound system. Carefully set focus and sound levels. The film should be carefully cued up and ready to go at the flip of a switch. We're all familiar with the academy leader (the strip that heads a movie: "Five-four-three-two-one"); don't make it part of your presentation. As we said, your audience has been conditioned to the standards of commercial television, so slip-ups like this are likely to lose you points.

Setting up a video requires similar care. You don't necessarily have to darken the room for short tapes, though for tapes of longer than two minutes you should, bringing the lights back up immediately after the tape finishes. Adjust the color and sound levels ahead of time. Clean the monitor screen if necessary. Every VCR and playback machine cues up a little differently. Leave your video accurately cued up with a second or two of black before the picture comes on. It should be left ready to go. If the playback unit has a remote control, know how to use it and make sure to locate it conveniently for easy use.

There's not much for you to do during the film or videotape presentation, but these media require careful introduction so that they support your presentation rather than take it over. Set up your audience using "flag" words to direct their attention: "Pay close attention to . . ." or "You'll notice about thirty seconds into this clip that . . ." These flag words cue the viewers in to what you want them to notice instead of randomly focusing on what interests them.

TIP: *Be aware that your audience will subconsciously judge film and video by the standards of commercial television — so they'd better be good.*

Handouts

Distributing printed copies of your presentation to the audience can help build retention. The key question is: When? Presenters who hand out copies before the presentation tell us that the scene is analogous to the movie *Field of Dreams*. The image from that movie was: "If you build it, they will come." Likewise for presentations: "If you hand it out, they will play." If you're prepared for the distraction of people flipping ahead or getting stuck on certain pages, handing out your presentation — or even key pages — can help you get your point across.

Handouts should reflect the shape of your presentation in content, and might well resemble your notes in form. As with any visual, take the trouble to execute handouts well. Make them clean and uncluttered; keep information to a minimum. Leave lots of white space around your key words or major points.

If you do decide to pass out your handouts before the presentation, you can make them an interactive part of your presentation by creating space for listeners to make notes. If people are taking notes, remember to slow down so they can get all the information.

> **TIP:** *One way to encourage people to take your handouts is to include something they might want to use later, such as the phone number of a particular public service you offer.*

NEW TECHNOLOGIES

Before this book comes off the printing press, new and improved presentation technologies will undoubtedly be available. Much of the use of this technology requires enhanced telephone/cable service to carry high speed transmission. Here are a couple of new ones to watch for.

Videofax — Videofax allows video, stills, text, images and sound to be sent to remote playback units. This can be used to announce upcoming events and welcome visitors to a location.

Computerized White Boards — One of the unique features of a white board is that it provides each presenter in a remote location with his/her own electronic ink to write on a touch-sensitive writing board. This technology works well when you need to modify charts and diagrams during a presentation. Just like any real-time presentation, make sure your handwriting is legible.

QUICK REFERENCE SUMMARY

- A presentation with visuals is 43 percent more persuasive than one without.
- Keep visuals simple and uncluttered, with a maximum of six lines per page.
- When in doubt, use fewer visuals rather than more.
- Phrases or words are better than sentences. Be consistent with structure throughout the visuals.
- Use color; it makes your visuals stronger.
- Try to limit visuals to one medium — except when you specifically design for multi-media.
- Pause before referring to information on visuals to allow the audience to absorb the visual.
- Put down the pointer when you're finished pointing out items. It's distracting to the audience if you hold it.
- When through explaining a visual, remove it.
- Flip charts are useful for small groups.
- Write charts in block capitals beforehand and use adequate spacing between lines.
- Overheads are useful for groups of up to fifty people.
- Use white borders for additional notes.
- Use the "striptease" technique when referring to lists on overhead. Show one point at a time to keep your audience focused.
- Laptop presentations require attention to viewing angles and knowing what the audience is seeing.
- Use TV monitors, LCD/overhead displays, or large screen projection with computer-generated graphics.
- 35-millimeter slides work well for ten to several hundred people.
- When using slides, tape the remote control to the side of the podium or lectern rather than holding it; this frees your hands to gesture. Tape over the reverse button to prevent hitting it accidentally.
- Film is good for any sized group; twenty-five people per videotape monitor is the maximum.

- Pre-focus projectors for smooth performance.
- Make sure there's a spare bulb for any projector.
- Film and videotape quality is judged by what is done commercially, so make it good.
- Use signal words to introduce visuals, such as, "Watch for . . ." or "You'll notice thirty seconds into this . . ." or "I want to emphasize the 3rd point on the next slide."
- Provide hard-copy handouts to increase audience retention. Distribute handouts after the presentation so the audience is not distracted, or if necessary to distribute handouts during the presentation, integrate them into the session and leave white space on handouts for audience to make notes.
- Use the correct visual medium for your presentation. Don't let it take over for you.

CHAPTER 9

Perfecting Delivery

In one important sense, a presentation is like a symphony: It may exist as notations on paper, but it really comes into being only through performance. And it's possible to perform a great work badly, just as it's possible to perform a mediocre one well. Beethoven's Fifth Symphony played by the New York Philharmonic is quite different from the same symphony played by the Springfield High School orchestra.

* * * * * *

Performance has an impact quite apart from the quality of the "work itself."

* * * * * *

The point here is that the *delivery* of your presentation, in a practical sense, is your presentation. Think about it. When you walk up to the front of that room you're a lot like an orchestra conductor stepping onto the podium. The unfolding of the event is in your hands. The content of your talk is already there in your notes — the musical score, so to speak — but without your skilled and sensitive execution it won't really work.

There's a cartoon we often share in our workshops: The drawing is of a little man in a tailcoat looking down at a large book laid out on the podium. There are no musical notes on the page, only an instruction telling the man to wave the baton until the music stops, then turn around and bow. We get a lot of laughs with this. That's how we all *wish* it were. In reality, however, it matters a lot what you do with the baton while you're up there. That's what this chapter is all about: the delivery skills you need to turn out a polished performance.

* * * * * *

Like it or not, how you look and sound has more impact on listeners than the actual words you speak.

* * * * * *

People don't carry away from a speech or presentation primarily information. They carry away an *impression.*

Let's look back for a moment to Chapter 1. Among the studies we quoted there is one that analyzes the dynamics of verbal communication. The findings:

- 55 percent of interpersonal communication comes from facial expression and other body language.
- 38 percent relates to "paralanguage," or vocal quality.
- The remainder — approximately 7 percent — is derived from the meaning of the words: the content.

* * * * * *

How you look and sound add up to 93 percent of the impression you make. And if those factors aren't working for you, they're working against you.

* * * * * *

We're not suggesting that content is unimportant. Skillful preparation of content is essential, which is why we've spent four chapters discussing it. But remember our chain analogy? The communications chain is no stronger than its weakest link. Like Beethoven's Fifth, your first-rate presentation content can be seriously undermined by poor delivery.

CASE STUDY: We once undertook to prepare an expert witness for testimony in a product liability lawsuit. The plaintiff in the case was a high school athlete who had injured his spine in a sports accident and was paralyzed as a result — possibly for life.

There were three defendants: the high school coach, the school board, and the manufacturer of the sports equipment the boy had been wearing. Our expert witness was an engineer testifying for the equipment manufacturer.

Juries like to award monetary "damages" in accident cases. In this case, the defendant most likely to be found responsible was our client, the equipment manufacturer. Not because they *were,* in fact, responsible, but because they had money — they were the "deep pocket."

The job of our key witness was to make the jury understand that the equipment was very carefully engineered and was as safe as it could possibly be. In his lab at the plant, the engineer was quite convincing about the careful design of the equipment. He made it quite clear to us that the equipment did an excellent job of protecting the head, but that it did not and could not protect the rest of the anatomy (in this case, the neck). Like many people who do not regularly testify, he was not comfortable in the courtroom, and despite his unquestionable expertise, he struck us as a potentially ineffective witness.

As might be expected of an inexperienced testifier, he spoke in a careful monotone: his voice was flat and evenly paced. He never gestured and he rarely looked at anybody while he spoke. He looked above everyone's head or down at the floor rather than meeting people's eyes.

He also used a lot of technical language in his answers. Although he was professionally correct in not wanting to oversimplify, we suggested he clarify his terms. It is important to understand that facts are facts, but in a court of law, facts are facts only if a jury (or judge) understands and believes them.

Once he accepted the idea that his role as a witness carried more importance than just conveying facts, he began to work on the presentation side of his testimony, as well. In any trial, it is up to the judge or jury to ultimately decide conviction or acquittal; however, as a result of our consulting, the witness and others from the company did come across better on the stand by improving eye contact, voice modulation, gestures, and using layman's English.

TIP: *The first words out of your mouth can set the tone for the audience. Practice eye contact, posture, pitch, volume and emphasis.*

* * * * * *

Content aside, what distinguishes the effective speaker is looking good and being intelligible.

* * * * * *

The two really cannot be separated. "Looking good" involves acting:

- Confident
- Animated
- Relaxed

These qualities are communicated through:

• Facial expression
• Eye contact
• Posture
• Physical gestures

"Being intelligible" — expressing yourself clearly and persuasively — involves sounding:

• Confident
• Animated
• Relaxed
• Articulate

These qualities are communicated through the elements of vocal inflection:

• Pace
• Pauses
• Pitch
• Volume

This, in turn, builds:

• Phrasing
• Emphasis

We'll discuss the role each of these elements plays in getting your message across, but first we'd like to offer some general facts and suggestions relating to appearance and impressions.

LOOKING GOOD

Whether we're aware of it or not, we begin communicating with our listeners even before we actually begin to speak. We think of communicating primarily as a process of moving our mouths, but how we move our bodies also speaks to our audience. How we stand, how we carry our head, where we rest our gaze, what we do with our hands — these are all components of language.

The impression-building process begins the instant a person becomes the focus of attention. The moment the image strikes their eyes, listeners will start forming impressions: "How attractive (unattractive) this man or woman is." "How authoritative (confident, intimidated, disorganized) he or she looks." "Look how tall (or short) he or she is, how trim (overweight)." "Look how much weight Leslie has lost since I last saw her." "What a nice blouse she's wearing." "Carl's tie is a little loud for this company." And so forth. All these impressions will have an effect on how the audience *listens*. To the extent that you can control the impressions you create, it is important to start on the right foot. (In this connection, see our discussion of presentation dress in Chapter 14.)

If you're at a lunch or a dinner, finish eating well before your presentation. Have your jacket buttoned; check your makeup; make sure your notes are ready; make whatever last-minute checks you need. If you're being introduced, be aware that the audience will not be concentrating on the person who's performing the introduction, they will be looking for the person being introduced.

So *be ready*. Model the behavior you want others to display when you're up there; look at the person who's introducing you; give that person the kind of attention you would like listeners to give you.

When the moment arrives to go on, stand up smartly — with good posture. Walk to the front of the room with a sense of purpose.

When you arrive, don't immediately begin speaking. Pause. Arrange your notes and visual aids. Get settled. Give the audience a moment to get used to you. Make eye contact. Smile. Then you can begin. This all adds up to an impression of conviction, authority, and self-assurance.

This nonverbal communication process continues for your entire presentation. It's subtle stuff, mostly taking place at the subconscious level. But it is powerful — and important enough to merit a detailed discussion of each of its elements.

When you're smilin'. . . The old song underlines an old truth: Smiling is infectious. So are the feelings it expresses. A smile from you, the presenter, is a positive signal to which your audience responds positively. It tells them you're comfortable — which makes them comfortable.

"Suppose I'm not comfortable?" Smile anyway. Two reasons. First, the reverse of what we said above is also true: If you communicate your discomfort to your listeners, it will make them uncomfortable. Second, and perhaps more important, smiling *will make you feel better*. This may strike you as absurd, but psychologists have discovered that while our faces naturally express what we're feeling inside, the reverse is also true to some extent. Our facial expressions — particularly the smile —

can actually alter our emotional chemistry. If you are afraid of flying, a smile will make you less uncomfortable in an airplane. If presentations make you nervous, a smile will make you feel more at home.

So we heartily recommend smiling. By "smile" we don't necessarily mean the expression used by actors in toothpaste commercials. A sphinx-like smile with the corners of the mouth turned up slightly is just fine — though you might want to flash a stronger version from time to time.

What the eyes tell. An image we like to use in teaching presentation skills is that communication is like a game of catch. When you throw a ball in a game of catch, you generally don't turn your back or bury your face in your hands, you look to see if the ball is caught. In the same sense, each time you toss out a thought or idea in your presentation, you should look to see if it is caught. You do this with eye contact. The catch is indicated by responses from individual audience members in the form of returned eye contact, a nod, a smile, or a generally attentive look. These responses let you know the ball has been caught and returned, and that the audience is awaiting the next toss. A good rule of thumb is that each thought, sentence, or idea is a separate throw and catch with another individual.

Eye contact will also tell you if your ball has not been caught (blank stares, no reaction, quizzical or uncomprehending looks) and this will alert you to stop and "throw again" (in other words, clarify your point) so that the game can continue.

Television has conditioned most of us to expect strong eye contact. The people who talk to us over the tube — be they newscasters, advertisers, or political speakers — look us straight in the eye (through the camera). So deeply are we conditioned that we subconsciously question the honesty and integrity — or at least the conviction — of anyone who will not or does not look us in the eye. This is basic practical psychology. By making *conscious* use of eye contact we can enhance the overall credibility and effectiveness of our presentation. Certainly, if we fail to make eye contact, we definitely limit the potential impact of our presentation.

If you doubt that people rely on eye contact to make impressions, think about your own personal experience. When you have something to say that you are consciously uncomfortable about in some way — if you're embarrassed or if you aren't telling the truth, for example — you tend to avoid the gaze of the person you're speaking to. And how do you know when children are lying? They won't look you in the eye.

Conversely, in a one-on-one situation where you have something earnest and important to convey, something you really want to get across — perhaps something as urgent as "I love you" — you actively seek out the other person's eyes.

It's not much different for public communication. Strong eye contact conveys an impression of confidence, conviction, openness, honesty, enthusiasm, even urgency. Poor eye contact may suggest anything from simple nervousness to embarrassment or furtiveness to outright mendacity.

Like smiling, eye contact says, "I'm comfortable with myself and with what I'm telling you." Avoidance of eye contact says, "There's something wrong here," leaving some part of the listener wondering, "Why doesn't this add up?"

This means not keeping your eyes glued to your notes — which suggests you are speaking from your own private bubble. It means not looking over the heads of the audience or off into the far reaches of space — which suggests that you are afraid of being with them. It means looking at the people you are talking to — at least a good part of the time. This may be somewhat unnerving at first. Why? For the very reason that it is important: It really is a gesture of intimacy.

Eye contact with whom, specifically? It generally doesn't matter a great deal with whom you make eye contact, simply that you look at someone. Exceptions are the question and answer session (see page 130), one-on-one presentations, and presentations in which a specific "power person" takes precedence over others. So it makes sense to pick a person who is giving you positive feedback such as a supportive nod or a smile. This should help to alleviate any discomfort you feel at fostering intimacy with utter strangers.

Here are three basic eye contact principles:

- In general, hold eye contact with a single person for at least a full thought, phrase, or sentence.
- In a group situation (except where you are obliged to play to a specific individual) divide the audience into several sections — like a tic-tac-toe board — in order to spread your eye contact around the group. The number of sections depends upon the size of the group. Pick a friendly face in each area. These people serve as your contact

points. You can then literally "work the room," moving from a friendly eye in one sector to a friendly eye in the next, returning as necessary. This grid solution works well for audiences of as few as six or as many as a thousand.

- In a one-on-one session, or when you're responding to a "power person," look directly at him or her and don't worry about the others very much.

> **TIP:** *If meeting people's eyes is a problem for you, try this trick: Rest your gaze on a person's forehead just above the eyebrows and visualize the Radio City marquee with the words of your text running across in lights.*

WINNING MOVES

Physical gestures are a vital ingredient in verbal communication.
Gestures do the following:

- Add emphasis to our words
- Animate the voice
- Provide an outlet for nervousness

If the words are the meat of communication, gestures are the spices. Gestures add flavor to our speech — the accents that make the difference between bland and stimulating.

Try a little test: Visualize yourself making an impassioned plea, speaking out urgently on a subject that you care about deeply — *without* gesturing — standing motionless with your arms at your sides. It's hard to picture, isn't it? Without gestures, half the message is lost. The same principle holds true for less impassioned utterances as well.

In addition, gestures have a direct effect on the voice, lubricating and animating it, making your speech more conversational and hence more accessible and more credible. You can actually "hear" your gestures when you listen to a tape recording of your presentation. Gesturing also tends to open up the upper body physically, promoting good breathing and muscular relaxation, both of which exert a further positive influence on the voice.

Perhaps most important of all, gesturing gives us a great way to burn off nervous energy. If we don't gesture, our nervousness finds other ways to express itself, usually ways that call attention to the nervousness, distracting our listeners and detracting from the impact of what we are saying.

> **TIP:** *Learn to gesture and you will live longer. We have seen studies reporting that orchestra conductors live longer than the average citizen. Why? Because in their work, the physical gesture is their sole means of communication. They are constantly using the arms and the upper body; more blood is pumped by the heart, taking more oxygen to the rest of the body. The result is better health and longer life — in addition to effective communications. We've already suggested, at the beginning of this chapter, that you think of yourself like an orchestra conductor; why not in this way as well?*

Helping gestures happen. Starting out in an appropriate stance can facilitate gesturing, and we recommend the "ski pole position." For those of you who don't ski, this means standing straight, forearms held at about waist level, with the hands apart, relaxed, and open. Most people find this a comfortable position from which it is easy and natural to gesture.

Stand up and try it. How does it feel? If having your hands "just hanging in space" feels awkward (which in itself should encourage you to gesture), try the "professorial" or the operatic "diva" position, in which the hands are brought together with the fingers lightly touching.

Problem postures. There are a number of postures that severely inhibit gesturing. An act as simple as clasping your hands together, for example, breeds a whole category of problem postures: the "firing squad" position — hands behind back, body often rocking forward and back; the LAPP "lower anatomical protective position" — hands anchored over the crotch; the HAPP "higher anatomical protective position," with arms crossed firmly over the breasts. There is nothing wrong with clasped hands, but having found something to hold on to (each other), the hands tend to remain firmly fastened together, effectively eliminating the possibility of gesturing.

Grasping the lectern creates similar problems. You've probably seen the "white knuckler," who appears to be holding on for dear life, and the "ship captain," who leans into the lectern and steers it first one way, then the other. Again, the problem is not that they grasp the lectern, but that they never let go. If you speak from a lectern, start with the hands resting *lightly* on it.

Whatever position you find yourself in, watch out for "sticky elbows," a position that is another serious inhibitor of gestures. Like hands, elbows seem to be provided with their own adhesive. If you start out with your elbows stuck to your sides, they are likely to remain there throughout your presentation. You will still be able to move your hands and forearms, but the gestures will tend to have a nervous, truncated quality.

Give it a try. Feels awkward, doesn't it? Your motions tend to be stunted and ungainly, as if you had seal flippers. Now unstick your elbows; immediately, your gestures become more fluid.

Some of you, of course, may be self-conscious about gesturing. Big, expansive gestures may feel quite unnatural. With all due respect, we feel that not gesturing is unnatural and that it's worth investing some of your time and energy to overcome your discomfort in this area. This is especially true if you are likely to be presenting to large groups in large spaces. In a big hall, the listeners at the back can't really see your face at all, but if you can make big gestures, they'll feel some sense of connection, even way back there. The bigger the room the bigger your gestures need to be.

With practice, gesturing will come to feel more natural. One good way to practice gesturing is to slip into your orchestra conductor persona and gesture on key words as you read dialogue from a book. If you have trouble remembering to gesture, put a little reminder symbol, perhaps a stick figure with arms upraised, or the word gesture next to key words in your notes.

More body problems. Two common unconscious physical habits that you should strive to avoid or eliminate are swaying or rocking back and forth and wagging your head from side to side, keeping time like the pendulum of a metronome. It's fine to shift your weight and to gesture with your head for emphasis, but the rhythmic repetition of either movement is distracting. It tends to give your speech a singsong cadence and conveys an overall impression of nervousness.

To combat swaying, try placing your feet either slightly closer together (to reduce your leverage), or slightly farther apart (to widen your base and stabilize the body), or with one foot slightly in front of the other. To combat head wagging, watch videotapes of your presentations and practice until you break the habit.

> **TIP:** *To remind yourself to gesture, use eye contact, watch for any bad habit, and pick a person in your audience to cue you for a certain thing. You might say, "When I look at Marge, I'll check to see if I'm swaying; when I look at Bill, that's a cue to check for eye contact."*

SOUNDING GOOD

If you have something to say that you believe in — if you are enthusiastic about what you do, your products, your research, the company you work for — your enthusiasm should be reflected in the way you speak as well as in the words you choose. Which brings us to "paralanguage" — vocal quality, or how we use our voices.

What most of us associate with the term *vocal quality* is the characteristic sound of an individual's voice — its unique tone or timbre: high, low; smooth, scratchy; breathy, resonant; nasal, guttural. These vocal characteristics are largely based on physical factors, but they can be changed far more than most of us realize. If you do not have a naturally pleasant voice and presentations are a necessary part of your life, you might consider devoting some time and effort to improving it by finding a voice teacher. There are many fine ones that teach speaking as well as singing.

In any case, there's a lot more to consider about vocal quality than timbre. Here we will explore the elements of inflection and their use to create phrasing and emphasis.

Inflection. The literal meaning of this word is "to bend, to alter." *Vocal inflection,* specifically, refers to voice variables:

- Pace
- Pauses
- Pitch
- Volume

We use these to make our verbalizations more expressive.

In comparison with that of other English speakers, American speech is characteristically deficient in inflection. Richness of inflection is one of the qualities that makes British (and other nonAmerican) English so distinctive — and so attractive. Fortunately, inflection is easy to improve, and once mastered will make your speech pleasant to listen to and easy to understand.

Pace. Fast, slow, or in between, words spoken at a steady, even pace take on a sameness, like driving through a prairie landscape. They blur together and soon lull the listener into inattention. Varying the pace of your words and phrases adds contour, creating interest.

It can be helpful to begin your talk at a somewhat slower pace than normal, especially if you are addressing people who are unfamiliar with your voice. This gives the audience time to "learn" your voice and speaking mannerisms. Once they have had a minute or two to get the hang of your style, you can step up the overall pace. This is a technique that Henry Kissinger uses for public speaking. He gives his listeners time to get used to his accent, then accelerates to his normal speaking pace.

* * * * * *

In some cases, speaking faster can actually increase comprehension.

* * * * * *

The brain can absorb information at rates up to approximately eight hundred words per minute — which is about four times faster than normal speech. Like a mainframe computer, the mind is spending only a small proportion of its time with the task of comprehension wanders, and concentration suffers. Dealing with a higher "word density," the mind of the listener is less likely to be distracted. The catch here, of course, is that if you want to speak quickly and be understood, you have to speak very clearly.

TIP: *Be strategic in how you vary your pace. In fact, slowing down or dropping in tone or volume, using signal phrases can help make your message stick.*

Another aspect of pace to consider is the changing of pace from phrase to phrase. We're not talking about anything contrived here, just using the natural rhythms of ordinary speech: Close your eyes and listen to any trained speaker, a good radio announcer, or even to an informal conversation. You'll discover that people — both professional speakers in their professional settings and non-professional in casual ones — group words together in "meaning clusters." They push together groups of relatively unimportant words and slow down to give emphasis to the key words and phrases that carry important information. It makes the words live.

We do this naturally, but when we get into a situation that's uncomfortable — speaking in front of a group of people, for example — we tend to freeze up and unnaturally even out our speaking pace. We can all spot an untrained or inexperienced person (like owners of small businesses who insist on doing their own television commercials) reading off a Teleprompter. The flat, mechanical singsong is unmistakable.

Pauses. Many presenters, especially inexperienced ones, are afraid to pause while speaking, even for a moment. To these people, two seconds of silence seems like an eternity. When asked to explain their reluctance to pause, our workshop clients often cite the fear that no communication is going on during the silence. This is simply not the case.

❋ ❋ ❋ ❋ ❋ ❋

Pauses are a vital element of nonverbal communication and are essential to strong delivery.

❋ ❋ ❋ ❋ ❋ ❋

We can't overemphasize this fact. Pauses contribute to communication in at least four ways:

1. They carry a message of their own ("I'm relaxed, thoughtful, and confident").
2. They serve as a catalyst for verbal comprehension by "ventilating" the flow of words. This gives the speaker time to catch his or her breath, and for the listeners to absorb what has been said.

❋ ❋ ❋ ❋ ❋ ❋

You should always pause following the introduction of a new key term or idea, and especially after displaying a visual.

❋ ❋ ❋ ❋ ❋ ❋

With terms or ideas, the pause can be brief; with a visual, it must be long enough for listeners to become readers and really take it in. This means two to three seconds.

3. Pauses also signal transitions. They say "Okay, we've finished that thought or topic; here comes the next point." Referring to your notes at these transition points seems natural and reinforces the message of the pause.

4. A brief pause in the middle of a phrase or sentence — in the "wrong place" — is a very effective way to call attention to what follows (see example, page 112).

Pitch and volume. We have a special word for speech that lacks this quality: monotone (literally, "one pitch"). It is clearly a pejorative term; we don't refer to someone's "stirring monotone." Used as an adjective, the word is monotonous — which means "boring" or "expressionless." Clearly, the rise and fall of vocal pitch is a key element in clear, communicative speech.

Always speaking at the same volume level is equally drab and expressionless. Both faults rob us of the opportunity to enhance the meaning of our words by directing the listeners' attention to what's important.

Phrasing and emphasis. In written communication, punctuation and typography are used as expressive devices to help to bring out the meaning of the words. In oral communication, clarity of expression is achieved through vocal inflection, as it creates phrasing and *emphasis*. And these add up to a much *more powerful* tool than commas, semicolons, and italics.

By the term *phrase* we don't mean quite the same thing a grammarian does. To a speaker, a phrase is an organizational unit, a "meaning cluster" — a group of words expressing a unified idea that is spoken in one breath. One thought equals one *breath* equals one *phrase*.

The natural lift that occurs after each phrase as we pause to take our next breath signals the listener that we have completed one idea or thought element and are about to start another. This creates what we call a "thought rhythm."

As an illustration, here's how the opening of Abraham Lincoln's celebrated Gettysburg Address might be phrased:

FOURSCORE AND SEVEN YEARS AGO [breath]
OUR FATHERS BROUGHT FORTH
  ON THIS CONTINENT [breath]
A NEW NATION [breath]
CONCEIVED IN LIBERTY [breath]
AND DEDICATED TO THE PROPOSITION [breath]
THAT ALL MEN ARE CREATED EQUAL.

Try it yourself. Read it out loud. For contrast, try running the phrases together without the lifts. (You should be able to read the lines in two breaths without much trouble.) Do it several times each way until you feel comfortable with the words. Which way do you prefer? Record your readings on tape and play them back. Which do you think would be easier for an audience to follow? We're betting on the shorter phrases. It is a documented fact that people speak in shorter word groupings than they write. The typical written sentence runs fifteen to twenty-three words; the average spoken sentence, eight to ten.

Emphasis. The complement to skillful phrase shaping is the careful placement of emphasis. To emphasize is, of course, to call attention to selected words or groups of words — to point to their special importance. But emphasis can add meaning as well.

> **TIP:** *If you're uncomfortable with short detached phrases, and feel unsure about how they really come across, rent a videotape of an old Bette Davis movie. Her phrasing really makes you pay attention — and you are never in doubt about what she's saying.*

Try this exercise. It is designed to make you aware of the subtleties of meaning that you can impart through emphasis. Say "I will not go" out loud four times, each time stressing a different word:

<u>I</u> will not go.
I <u>WILL</u> not go.
I will <u>NOT</u> go.
I will not <u>GO</u>.

Each reading conveys a slightly different message. The first is about the identity of who will go; maybe somebody else but not me. The rest are variations on an emphatic statement, but with different connotations. The second suggests stubbornness in the face of urging. The third is a flat contradiction. The last, a defiant proclamation — the most emphatic of all.

Emphasis can be achieved by means of any or all of the elements of vocal inflection we examined earlier:

Changing pace or pausing. One simple and effective way to emphasize an important word is to pause briefly before enunciating it. For example: "The plan that has been proposed this morning is . . . a disaster." This is especially effective when combined with changes in pitch and volume.

Changing pitch. Just as a monotone signals the listener that there is nothing of special importance in what you are saying, inflecting your vocal pitch clearly creates interest. It doesn't much matter whether the pitch change is upward or downward, except at the end of sentences, where consistent downward inflection suggests a lack of conviction.

Changing volume. Speaking louder is perhaps the most obvious way to create emphasis, but *decreasing* the volume is actually just as effective. It is the contrast that creates the emphasis. A whispered phrase can be very dramatic.

As you prepare a presentation, you can plan your phrasing and placement of emphasis in portions of the talk that are important enough to write out. Expand on the technique we used earlier in our Gettysburg Address example. Write or type each phrase on a separate line; then simply underline the words you wish to emphasize. Which words should you emphasize? The active, emotional ones; these will generally be verbs, nouns, and adjectives.

```
FOURSCORE AND SEVEN YEARS AGO
OUR FATHERS BROUGHT FORTH
   ON THIS CONTINENT
A NEW NATION
CONCEIVED IN LIBERTY
AND DEDICATED TO THE PROPOSITION
THAT ALL MEN ARE CREATED EQUAL.
```

TIP: *We don't want to leave the subject of emphasis without extending an urgent plea: Try to avoid the cliché, now solidly embedded in our aural culture by second-rate television news broadcasters and public officials, of stressing the prepositions (such as of, to, for, in, among). It is a verbal affectation that adds nothing useful to your speech. Also, don't stress conjunctions (and, but, because) and articles (a, an, the).*

Here are a few general rules about delivery:

- Any time you pose a question — even a rhetorical one — make a real pause. Whether or not you expect listeners to answer, it lends emphasis and gives them time to consider the implications.
- Avoid the habit of letting the ends of your sentences drop. If you have this problem, practice deliberately emphasizing the final two or three words of every sentence until this becomes second nature.

  To listeners, this mannerism suggests a lack of conviction. It often *occurs* for an entirely different reason: either because your mind is already onto the next sentence or thought, or because you are running out of breath. If the former, remember to pause and slow down; if the latter, practice speaking in shorter phrases, remembering to pause and *breathe*.
- Never undermine your selling points by glossing over them vocally. Be fully aware that you are delivering a selling point and stress it. "Signal" words, like *proud* or *excited*, what's significant, can help to add appropriate emphasis.
- If you feel a verbal fumble coming on, ask your audience's permission to stop and think. You can cover with a phrase like, "Let me consider how best to say this. . . ."
- Take care to enunciate key words clearly, especially trade names and terms, and most especially if there's any ambiguity. If you're discussing UNIX (an operating system for computers), for example, you don't want half your audience to be wondering why on earth you are talking about emasculated harem attendants (eunuchs). If any such verbal gremlin is lurking in your presentation, make sure the audience sees the word written down right off the bat.

PRACTICE GUIDELINES

All the elements of vocal quality can be readily improved through practice. The first step is to attune your ear. You can build your awareness of pace, pitch, and volume inflection just by carefully listening. Many study materials are readily available, from television and radio to the conversation going on behind you in a restaurant. Close your eyes, and don't even listen to the words. Just hear the speeding up and slowing down, the placement of pauses, the rise and fall of the voice, the changes from loud to soft, the emphasis of an important phrase.

Then practice. Take a section of your presentation that's well worked out — your opening, for example. Write it out as we suggested above — in short phrases divided into logical units of meaning. Decide which words to emphasize in order to best express your message, and underline them. Read the lines out loud using different types of emphasis: upward inflection and downward, louder and softer. Mark your pauses.

Once you begin to be comfortable with your expanded range of expression, record yourself on tape. While this will probably increase your self-consciousness at first, the direct feedback will be invaluable in helping you fine-tune your handling of inflection and emphasis. Eventually it will become second nature, and in time it will evolve into a distinctive personal speaking style.

QUICK REFERENCE SUMMARY

- Good delivery or performance can enhance content. Poor delivery or performance can *undermine* content.
- An audience carries away an impression of you that can outweigh the content of what you say.
- How you look and sound constitutes 93 percent of the impression you make.
- Three components of effective delivery are:
  — Confidence
  — Animation
  — Relaxation

- The audience begins judging and evaluating you the minute you're introduced — before you even open your mouth. Be ready.
- Walk to the front of the room with dignity and authority. Posture is critical in making a good impression.
- Pause and survey the room before you begin speaking; pick out friendly faces.
- Smile as you begin your talk.
- Look at the audience as you speak. Stop talking to look down at your notes, then look up and resume.
- Keep your eyes on one person for a full thought, or a complete sentence.
- If you have trouble meeting people's eyes, look at a person's nose or forehead; this creates the illusion of eye contact.
- Making eye contact with the audience helps relieve your own anxiety.
- Gestures are important in presentations. They burn off tension naturally, animate your face, and lubricate your voice.
- When using a lectern, don't lean on it in order to press tension away. Keep your hands at waist level and allow yourself to gesture naturally.
- Use variety in your voice; pause, alter your pitch for emphasis and phrasing.
- Speak important phrases slowly.
- Pause to let the audience absorb information. This lets you emphasize a point nonverbally.
- Use signal words to introduce an important phrase. Deliver the phrase, then pause. This helps people remember.
- Vary your pitch for emphasis.
- Speaking in a quiet, confidential tone is a strong way to occasionally make a point.
- Keep phrases short, so you can deliver them in one breath. Eight to ten words per sentence is appropriate.
- Analyze your text to mark for emphasis. Stress can alter the meaning of your content.

Tough Questions, Good Answers

Usually, the most effective format for making your point is a brief talk or presentation *followed by a question and answer period*. The experienced presentation-maker knows this well and will insist on a Q & A whenever possible.

* * * * * *

Properly handled, a Q & A session gives you an opportunity to make your point again — often several times.

* * * * * *

Furthermore, in many situations — internal presentations, witness appearances, and interviews, for example — answering questions is mandatory. The personnel manager, customer, divisional vice president, regulatory commissioner, concerned community member, opposing counsel, or reporter will *ask* any question. Their questions may be tough — and your answers had better be good. That's what this chapter is about: tough questions and good answers.

You can see that the art of handling questions is a crucial component of the presenter's craft. Although many people find the prospect intimidating, rest assured that it consists of a set of skills that you can learn.

* * * * * *

If you do the considerable amount of work involved in mastering Q & A skills, you can transform a potentially terrifying prospect into an important opportunity.

* * * * * *

Mastery of Q & A doesn't mean you can entirely eliminate the risks involved in facing questions. Mastery is primarily a matter of preparation, and you can never be prepared for *every* question. You may still get a zinger or a dumb, off-the-wall question from time to time. But if you've been through our Q & A training and are comfortable with the techniques of handling questions, you'll have a huge advantage. You'll be equipped to handle these situations with equanimity and, frequently, to *turn them to your advantage.*

If we haven't already made it clear, we believe that the Q & A is the most important part of the presentation process. There are four reasons, all of them related to retention.

1. This is the first time listeners have had an opportunity to actively participate in an exchange of ideas or information.
2. You can reemphasize important points.
3. You can introduce new, positive information.
4. The last things heard are remembered best.

The first reason Q & A helps you make your point is that interacting with the speaker is stimulating to the audience; it makes them *focus their attention* better. They will actually remember your message better when it's presented as an answer to *their* questions than when you make the same point in your prepared talk.

The second is that it gives you an opportunity to repeat. Repetition is one of the factors that increases retention. The more often your listeners hear a message, the more likely they are to remember it.

The third reason is that a question often creates an opportunity for you to deliver a selling point that didn't quite fit in with your talk, thus allowing you to make one of your main points again in a different way.

Point four really speaks for itself. There's one final benefit of the Q & A. It gives you an opportunity to display you. Some even suggest Q & A gives you a chance to show off. In the context of a Q & A, your energy, confidence, conviction — and in the face of difficult or hostile questioning, your courage and compassion — have a better chance to come through than they do from behind the lectern. All of which helps you *get to the point.*

THE CONTROL FACTOR

A lot of people find the idea of the Q & A unnerving. The reason? They feel that in taking questions they relinquish control. With the opening portion of your presentation — the "prepared text" — you are in command. You choose the words and the pictures, and direct the flow of ideas. But when the time comes to throw the floor open to discussion — if you know that the vice president, the comptroller, or whoever, may interrupt you at any moment — you may feel like a tiny boat on a storm-tossed sea, completely at the mercy of the elements. In reality, you can retain a considerable degree of control when the presentation becomes interactive.

> **CASE STUDY:** During his White House years, Henry Kissinger, undoubtedly one of the most successful communications manipulators of recent times, once reportedly opened a press conference by asking the press corps, "Does anyone have questions for my answers?" His quip made explicit what he knew and the reporters knew: For Henry Kissinger a press conference was more than a place to answer questions; it was an opportunity to deliver prepared policy statements on issues of his own choosing. They did ask questions, and he did provide answers, but he in no way relinquished the agenda to the press. He went in knowing what points he wanted to make — and he made them.

❋ ❋ ❋ ❋ ❋ ❋

Skilled Q & A handling is a process of turning questions — as often as possible — into a platform for remaking your points.

❋ ❋ ❋ ❋ ❋ ❋

Mr. Kissinger's press conferences illustrate the basic point we wish to make — that you don't have to relinquish control. However, we don't suggest that you imitate Mr. Kissinger's outspoken style of handling the matter. When you're in that powerful a position, go right ahead. Meanwhile . . .

❋ ❋ ❋ ❋ ❋ ❋

The best overall effect is achieved when you are responsive to the questions and keep your awareness of the control factor in the background.

❋ ❋ ❋ ❋ ❋ ❋

BE PREPARED

The Q & A technique we will outline is one of answering the questions and then finding a connection between that question and one of your selling points. The key to Q & A control is *preparation*. This point can't be overstressed. So before we work through the technique let's spend some time preparing.

✳ ✳ ✳ ✳ ✳

> *In Q & A, there's virtually no such thing as being overprepared.*

✳ ✳ ✳ ✳ ✳

Phase One of preparation is, specifically, preparation for difficult *questions*. This begins back where we started — with the audience profile. Remember our potential conflict analysis? That's the part of the audience profile that relates specifically to Q & A. It's a clue to the kinds of questions you can expect.

If you're prepared for a question, you're obviously going to do a better job of handling it.

CASE STUDY: Marlin Fitzwater, press secretary to President's Reagan and Bush, has said the White House staff can anticipate roughly four out of five questions reporters will pose at any given press conference. This means that during the press conference, the President is ready for 80 percent of the questions that come from the floor.

If the President of the United States can anticipate four out of five questions in an unrestricted presidential press conference, then with preparation the rest of us ought to be able to anticipate nine out of ten questions.

This means that roughly one time in ten someone will throw you a curve when you were looking for a fastball, and you will have to think on your feet. It also means that the rest of the time you'll have an answer prepared. You'll know what's coming — maybe not the exact words or all the nuances, but at least the specific area or issue. And you'll be able to step into the pitch and hit a line drive up the middle.

In other words, contrary to appearances, a skilled handler of Q & A is never very far from his or her "prepared text," because that text includes answers for every question that might come up.

The first step in your preparation is to anticipate, write down, and think through every question that might come up in the context of your topic. Look especially for difficult, tricky, or belligerent ones. Then prepare answers as far in advance as possible.

* * * * * *

This is the most rigorous work you will have to do in the course of your presentation training. But, like a lot of what a recruit does in boot camp, it will pay off under fire. Walking into a Q & A without doing this homework is like walking into battle without a weapon.

* * * * * *

For this exercise, we recommend you make a *Difficult Questions Worksheet.* The worksheet is essentially a four-part list containing:

- Questions you have found difficult to answer in the past
- Questions on matters you would prefer not to have exposed in public, to other departments, to your superiors, or to interviewers
- Issues that are particularly critical to your position, department, business, industry, or organization
- Your primary selling points

After making out your Difficult Questions Worksheet, spend some time mulling over the contents. This is not a process you want to hurry through. If possible, spread it out over several days. Try to expand your thinking. Don't always be linear; let your mind associate freely. Consider every possible ramification of your business, of related public concerns, and of your positive program. Continue this process — letting ideas percolate and integrate — until you feel you really know your way around all the issues, pro and con.

TIP: *Try the Mind Mapping technique for Q & A. Write the central themes for the Q & A in the middle of the page and write down sub-ideas and questions around it.*

By the time you've completed this phase of preparation, you should be pretty comfortable with a broad spectrum of questions. *Part* of your job in the Q & A will be to answer those questions, but it's not your whole job. Along with your answers, you also want to work in your selling points. That's what makes the Q & A an *opportunity*.

Phase Two of preparation is the forging of connections between the issues raised by the questions you studied in phase one and your selling points. For help in this second phrase of preparation, we have designed the *Minus/Plus Worksheet* (see next page).

On the left side of the page, list all the negative issues; on the right **side,** list all your positive selling points. As you study the material in this format, your aim is to *bridge* the rhetorical space that separates the two sides with concepts that create a connection between one side and the other. Look for logical paths that lead from items on the negative side to items on the positive side and draw actual lines connecting issues that relate conceptually.

Sometimes you can answer a minus question with a plus word and specifics. For example, **Question:** "Isn't this promotional plan unnecessary?" **Answer:** "It's *absolutely* necessary. Let me give you our specific objective and our anticipated results."

Sometimes you need to answer the negative and use a "but" or a "however" to get to your plus side. For example, **Question:** "Isn't the anticipated expense figure 1.5 million dollars with only a three hundred thousand dollar sales figure the first year?" **Answer:** "Yes, that's true. *But* this is an investment that will make us competitive in the long run. The numbers show us turning a profit in the fourth year."

❀ ❀ ❀ ❀ ❀ ❀

Work out a connection from every item on the minus side to some point on the plus side. It's much more important for all the minuses to be covered than for every plus to make an appearance.

❀ ❀ ❀ ❀ ❀ ❀

You will probably begin to notice that certain concepts crop up more often than others (the cost of living or the importance of customer service, for example). These are your "higher" or "broader" issues; take special note of them because they are important.

MINUS/PLUS WORKSHEET

– – – – –	+ + + + +

Q & A ARCHITECTURE: BUILDING BRIDGES

After analyzing in detail how "their" questions and "your" answers connect, you're now ready to meld these two elements into the powerful rhetorical device we call the *bridging technique.*

As the name suggests, the technique consists of building a verbal bridge between the point raised by the questioner and the selling point you *wish to emphasize.*

CASE STUDY 1: A classic example of skillful bridging is drawn from the 1980 presidential campaign when candidate Edward Kennedy appeared on a television interview program.

The senator's pet campaign issue was his health care program for the elderly and it was a popular issue. His selling points were bankable votes for him, so naturally he wanted to make the audience aware of it. Twenty minutes of the thirty-minute program had gone by and the senator hadn't had an opportunity to talk about health care. The next question was: "Senator, what is your view on the MX missile?"

Think for a moment what you would do in this situation. You need to answer the question, but you also need to get in some of your selling points. Is there any way that you can answer the question and find a connection that will allow you to bridge to health care? How about the issue of costs?

Senator Kennedy's answer went something like this: "My staff and I are against the MX. We don't think it is the right weapons system for this country. First of all, we are adequately covered by our existing systems. Second, you can't look at the MX — or any other weapons system — without focusing on its cost. We have only so much money in our national budget. I believe that more funds should be spent on domestic priorities such as rebuilding our roads or in areas such as national health care . . ."

With this bridge, Kennedy was off and running. "In this country today, the average American senior citizen spends about one-third of his or her income for health care maintenance. With my bill, we can bring this down to one-fifth or less, and each elderly person in this town could save as much as four hundred dollars a year."

At this point, the reporters might follow up with further questions on the health care issue, or they might come back to the MX missile. The point is that the smooth transition gave the senator a chance to make his selling point and left him in a position where it was even odds he would be able to make others.

That's the technique in a nutshell. Here was a smooth, logical, persuasive path from the *issue* of a weapons system; to the *broader issue* of costs and the national budget, to a *specific economic issue* — the high cost of health care. And finally the *selling* point — the Kennedy-sponsored bill and its benefits for the elderly.

CASE STUDY 2: Moving to the private sector, as vice president in charge of public relations for Goldome, Marc Chodorow was talking to a reporter on the subject of KWIKLINE, the bank's telephone banking service.

"Twenty-five to thirty percent of our 'platform' transactions [at a desk, with an officer] are now being handled by phone . . ." he was saying when the reporter broke in: "Does this mean that old-fashioned, face-to-face human services are going down the tubes?"

"Not at all," said Chodorow. "We still believe in personal banking services, and we always will, but *[but* is often a very important word in bridging] we find that using the phone works better for us — it's cheaper and more efficient. And frankly, it often works better for our customers as well.

"Here's an example. Last April 15, just hours before the last possible minute to file a tax return, we got a call from a customer who was out of town but who wanted to fund his IRA. The added complication was that he needed to take out a loan to do so. We were able to take care of both transactions for him over KWIKLINE in time for him to meet the IRS filing deadline."

The story makes another textbook example of skillful bridging: Chodorow answered the question (we aren't abandoning walk-in banking services), bridged (but) to his selling point (we think it works better — for us and for the customer), and added a memorable supporting specific (look what this service can do for you in a pinch).

Bridging is a flexible and adaptable technique that can be used one way or another in almost any Q & A situation. The more you do it, the better you'll be at it.

PRACTICE, PRACTICE, PRACTICE

We have a whole chapter on practicing, but practice is particularly crucial for Q & A, so we need to say a few things about it here.

Skillful Q & A always requires specific preparation. Former President Reagan reportedly spent approximately six and a half hours preparing for every press conference. That's the kind of commitment that produces results. But before you get into that league, you're going to have to devote some time to mastering the pivotal Q & A technique—bridging.

Your practice at this stage has three primary goals:

- Perfection of your command over the issue-bridge-selling point links
- A spontaneous conversational tone
- Conciseness

The more closely you can approximate real presentation conditions, the more effective your practice will be. This means responding to real questions. Getting a friend, spouse, or colleague to scan your worksheet and fire tough questions at you would be most effective. if you don't have access to a practice partner, you will have to frame questions for yourself — just as you imagine they might come from the audience:

- Write your questions down on slips on paper.
- Put the slips in a paper bag and pull them out one by one to simulate random questions from an audience.
- Do not write down your answers. Say them out loud, in your own words, just as you would in any conversation or discussion.

As you practice, *strive to refine and simplify your answers.* The more succinct they are, the more likely they are to be understood and re-tained. Work at getting the main message of your selling point as close to the front of your answer as possible.

Repeat each answer until it goes smoothly. This will probably take you about three tries per answer in the beginning. As you develop skill, you'll do better and better on your first try.

To really help yourself improve, record your practice sessions on audio tape. Listening to yourself speak is the most effective feedback.

As you listen to the tapes of your practice session, we suggest that you first make notes on what you like, then concentrate on what needs improvement.

MORE Q & A TECHNIQUES

You've prepared for the tough questions and spent time practicing the bridging technique. You're probably feeling pretty confident about the prospect of facing a question and answer session.

We've got some good news and some bad news. The bad news is that you're not quite ready yet; there are more question-handling techniques for you to master. The good news is that they're easy — and they will make your performance that much stronger.

The following rules and guidelines will keep the Q & A session running smoothly and under your control. They will help you steer clear of serious pitfalls, and generally help to make your Q & A a success.

Keep in mind that these are generalities and must be filtered through experience and common sense. Some points are more applicable to one situation than another. The list is most useful in the more formal presenter/audience situation. In the one-on-one meeting with your boss, or in a job interview, you are much more restricted in the range of appropriate techniques.

Set ground rules. In small presentations, this is not usually possible. In large meetings, however, this is highly recommended to establish your authority in the Q & A setting.

You may, for example, ask that questioners raise their hands or stand and identify themselves and their affiliations. You will probably want to save questions until after you have completed your presentation. If so, ask listeners to hold their questions until the end. If you want to limit questions to one per person and a follow-up, say so; you can always graciously make an exception to this or any ground rule on an ad hoc basis. If you forget to ask members to hold their questions and someone interrupts, either suggest that he or she write down the question and save it until the end, or you can answer it and ask everyone else to please hold further questions until you have finished your presentation.

Be prepared to get the ball rolling. When preparing for a Q & A session, you should always write a question or two *for yourself*. Audiences are sometimes slow to begin asking questions and you must start the ball rolling or the whole Q & A may fall flat.

"One question that is frequently raised about this subject is . . ." is one way to handle it. Another is, "Just before we started this evening, Marty asked me . . ." There are many possibilities. Once you have primed the pump, the audience will generally warm up and begin asking their own questions.

> **TIP:** *You can help stimulate questions from the audience while you set your ground rules: As you explain how you'd like members of the audience to seek recognition, raise your arm to illustrate; you'll find that this tends to elicit an arm-raising response. If this doesn't do the trick, proceed to your fall-back questions.*

Answer all questions. Only personal questions, questions relating to proprietary information, and questions to which you don't have answers (see our discussion of "I don't know" questions on page 133) are exceptions. The rest are fair game.

Try to look at difficult questions as an opportunity to demonstrate your strength. If questions have been submitted in written form, you might consider tackling one or two of the tough ones first just to demonstrate your willingness to face all issues. Here is an opportunity to head off anticipated questions raising particular problems. If you have prepared conscientiously, you should be able to offer a reasonably strong answer to the occasional unpredictable zinger. And even if you don't handle a question brilliantly, the courage and commitment you show by taking it on in good faith will ultimately work in your favor.

Always pause before answering a question. Pausing gives you time to collect your thoughts. It takes the brain more than two seconds to formulate a well-considered answer, and when the question is a difficult one, you really need that think time. The pause helps you avoid the pitfalls of "having your tongue drive your brain" and unconsciously repeating the negative language in a hostile or inflammatory question (which we will discuss presently). Just remember: Listen, think, and answer.

Not all questions are brain-crunchers, but there are two good reasons to pause *even on easy questions.*

First, the pause conveys an attitude of respect both for the questioner and for the question itself. It tells the audience that you are relaxed and that you regard each question as worthy of serious reflection. It also shows that you are *listening.* Jumping on the question before it is out of the questioner's mouth is likely to send the message either that you are anxious or that you have glib, readymade answers for everything.

Second, if you pause before *every* question, the audience quickly assimilates this as an aspect of your style. Then when you are asked the tough question and you *need* the time, your pause doesn't telegraph to the audience the message that you find the question a problem.

For difficult questions, in addition to pausing, it is a good idea to have a small repertoire of phrases prepared to extend your time to think. This will also allow you to launch into your answer unobtrusively. ("Well, let me tell you how we view that issue. . . .") Try to avoid the response, "I'm glad you asked that question," which often comes across as defensive. On the other hand, an acceptable answer, even on the witness stand, is, "I've never thought about the issue that way. Give me a moment to consider it in that light."

Bridge answers whenever possible. With innocuous questions, bridge to your selling points. With tricky or embarrassing questions, after dealing with at least part of the substance, bridge away to more comfortable ground. Respond to the specifics of the question and move to the realm of the larger issues that it raises. Once there, you can almost always reiterate your message.

Don't repeat negative language. A natural response to a tough question is to buy time to think by repeating the question verbatim. This is the worst thing you can do. In mindlessly repeating the question, you will be emphasizing the negatively charged language. ("Are we ripping off the public with our new pricing structure? . . .")

Coming full circle to repeat a question at the end of an answer is a natural impulse. If you do not check it, especially with a hostile or otherwise difficult question, you may undo a lot of skillful work you did in bridging away from it in the first place. You may well end up where your questioner began — with a negative statement. ("So, no, in answer to your question, I don't think we're ripping off the public . . .") You want to end with the positive. It might help to visualize a bridge — a structure that leads from one side of the river to the other, not around in a circle. (See page 135 for a case study.)

Anticipate the brain-crunchers. To defuse a potentially volatile issue — if you suspect or know that someone in the group is going to hit you with a tough question — you can meet it head-on by raising it yourself. It certainly is better for you to do this than for you to be surprised with it from the floor. And the audience may respect you for your courage and candor.

Keep it moving. Make an effort to be crisp and concise with your answers. In general, aim at keeping your answers between thirty seconds and a minute. Answer the question; if appropriate, bridge to a selling point; take another question.

Disengage eye contact and move to another questioner. This helps you include more people in your answers and also discourages follow-ups. Establish eye contact as you field a question. Maintain that contact for the first few moments of your answer. Then shift to one or more other members of the group, perhaps settling on the next questioner even as you finish your current answer.

This technique obviously doesn't apply when you're dealing with a power person. You must stick with that person until he or she is done dealing with the question or issue.

Leave on a high note or with a brief summary. Nothing looks worse than dutifully droning on until the audience has no more questions. After the Q & A time you have allotted, or when you feel you've reemphasized your selling points, you should wind up the session. An effective technique is to ask for "one or two more questions." If the first is an easy one and you have made a positive bridge on your answer, you can use that as an opportunity to exit. If you don't manage to handle the first question smoothly, take a second. If neither goes particularly well, give a prepared thirty-second summary of your presentation so that you can leave the audience with a positive message. You might actually say, "Although I didn't handle that question particularly well, let me finish strongly with a brief summary."

Close with dignity. Following your final answer or your summary statement, pause for a count of two or three, take off your microphone, gather your papers, and walk off with the same purpose and dignity with which you approached the lectern.

QUICK REFERENCE SUMMARY

- "Q & A session" doesn't mean "inquisition"; use it to your advantage.
- Preparation is the key to feeling in control of the Q & A.
- Analyzing the audience is the number one priority.
- Anticipate and practice difficult questions.
- Use the bridging technique to turn negative questions into positive answers.
- Try "Mind Mapping" — free association of ideas emanating from the central thought of a question — to allow you to bridge to a selling point.
- Develop the discipline of using the Minus/Plus Worksheet. It will help you create transitions from negative questions to positive answers.
- By bridging you can (1) narrow the focus of interest of a question to a specific issue within the issue raised, or (2) expand the focus of interest to the broader issue, which may allow you to bring in selling points.
- Bridging can diffuse an adversarial question.
- It is important to answer a question first, then bridge.
- To practice Q & A, have a friend ask tough questions. If no help is available, write questions on slips of paper, and draw them at random.
- Always pause before answering a question. Take time to think.
- First thought when a question comes is "What's my selling point?" Second thought: "What's my bridge?" Pause. Then answer.
- In many cases, you can set ground rules. When possible, make things as comfortable for yourself as you can.
- To stimulate questions, ask one of yourself.
- Don't dodge or evade questions. If you don't know the answer, say so and volunteer to get the information to the questioner.
- When you don't know the answer to a question, try to bridge back to something pertinent that you do know.
- Watch for negative language in questions. Never repeat negative language in your answer.

- Don't repeat questions — unless the audience really can't hear them.
- In an adversarial encounter, move your eyes to another questioner as you finish your answer. This prevents follow-ups.
- If possible, keep answers short. Thirty seconds to a minute is appropriate.
- Leave on a high note. Always summarize key points in a positive manner.

Tricky Questions, Difficult Questioners

Most questions are straightforward, inviting equally straightforward answers. But there are several types of questions containing rhetorical pitfalls that come up frequently enough so that every presenter needs to learn to recognize them immediately.

The same holds true for several types of questioners (or styles of questioning) that have a disruptive effect on the smooth flow of your Q & A.

In examining these problems, we will concentrate on two separate but related areas:

Awareness: Learning to identify the specific types of problems.

Tactics: Learning how to deal with them smoothly, maintaining focus and control, and turning potential problems into *opportunities* to make your point.

TRICKY QUESTIONS

The "I Don't Know" Question

For some reason, many of us feel when we get up in front of a group we have to be omniscient; as a result, we are often reluctant to acknowledge our occasional ignorance.

* * * * * *

Sometimes, the best answer you can give to a question is, "I don't know."

* * * * * *

If you don't know the answer, don't make it up. Trying to fake an answer is a mistake for several reasons:

- It's hard to be convincing when you're not convinced yourself.
- If there is someone present who does know the answer, you're likely to be shown up on the spot.
- If anyone in the audience later learns that your answer was incorrect, you may look bad forever in that person's view, no matter how well you handled yourself during the Q & A.

If you don't know, *step one* is be candid; say so.

But don't leave matters there. *Step two* is to amplify; offer whatever explanation or justification you can: "I'm sorry, that just isn't my area of expertise" or "Those figures won't be available for another few days."

Step three is always to offer to remedy the situation: "I'll find out that information and get back to you. When will you need that by?"; "See me afterward and I'll tell you whom to contact about this"; or, to a reporter, "What's your deadline?"

Step four, having demonstrated your integrity and good faith, is to transform this into an opportunity. By bridging back to what you do know, you create an opportunity to deliver a selling point: "But I can tell you that in this general area we've been making an effort to . . ." This response is like a negotiation where you say, "I can't give you that, but will you take this instead?"

The Loaded or Negative Question
Confrontational questions that contain highly charged negative language ("rip-off," "monopoly," "profiteering," "endangering public health") can be very disconcerting. Saying little is your best tactic in response.

* * * * * *

Never reinforce negative or highly charged language in a question by repeating it.

* * * * * *

You may not be able to neutralize the effect of such a question entirely, but don't lend credence to the charge by expanding on it.

Take your time. Pause. Use your own words. Above all, be concise. Don't over-answer and don't allow yourself to get drawn in or distracted by the emotionality of what's been said.

If you need to buy a little extra thinking time, use a phrase like, "I certainly wouldn't use those words," or "I strongly disagree with your characterization . . ."

CASE STUDY: Former President George Bush was well schooled in the bridging technique. However, in one memorable example, he lost the "battle" with a reporter's question by repeating the negative language in a question. Early in his administration, a reporter asked the President a question: "What's your reaction to charges that your administration is in *drift* and there's a certain *malaise* in the White House?" While Bush spent most of his time on the "plus" side of the *Minus/Plus* analysis sheet, he ended up with newspaper headlines he didn't want. In denying the premise in the question, Mr. Bush said: "I disagree, I don't see any drift, I don't see any malaise . . ." While Mr. Bush then *bridged* to positive information, the damage was done. The headlines in the newspaper the next day were: "Bush denies drift . . .", "Bush sees no malaise." The better tactic would have been a denial like: "I can't agree with those charges. What I would say is . . ."

The Forced Choice (aka the False Choice)

This is the situation in which the questioner poses two alternatives as if they were mutually exclusive ("Do you walk to school, or do you carry your lunch?") and invites the presenter to endorse one or the other.

* * * * * *

The real answer to an "A or B" question may well be "neither A nor B, but C." Or it may be "both A and B."

* * * * * *

("Are lower earnings the result of mismanagement or employee theft?" Quite possibly neither one. "What do you want, high profits or a clean environment?" Without question, both.)

The defense against the forced choice is simple: Awareness. As long as you recognize the critter when it turns up, it is easy enough to deal with: Remember to pause thoughtfully, then use the word *both or neither,* as the occasion requires.

The Multiquestion

Often when people get an opportunity to ask a question they sense that this may be their only chance. Typically, they then turn all the various questions on their mind into one lengthy run-on question. Trying to log in, remember, and respond to a whole list of questions can be confusing, taxing, and time consuming.

This is one situation in which it is okay not to be 100 percent responsive.

● ● ● ● ●

If you ask the questioner which question he or she wants you to answer first, it invariably turns out to be the toughest.

● ● ● ● ● ●

Instead, simply pick out the one question that you most want to answer and do it. Everyone is generally satisfied with this. A second option is to respond along these lines: "Well, you've asked me several questions; I think the issue that covers all of them is . . ."

The situation where these tactics don't work is the small management meeting or any other one-on-one situation where you're being grilled by your superiors. In this type of Q & A session it's best to reply succinctly. Take notes as questions are asked, then try to answer them. If you need to buy a little think time, you can ask for a restatement of one or more questions, or a confirmation of specific items asked for. It is okay to be human in this situation; if you forget one of the questions, it's all right to ask: "What was your third question again?"

In terms of the order in which you answer multiple questions from your boss, if there is a particularly tough one, you might choose to tackle that one first. This allows you to move on to more comfortable territory and end your multi-answer on a positive note.

The Hypothetical Question

Many questioners begin their queries with "Suppose that . . ." or "What if . . ." and then, describing some particular set of circumstances, invite you to speculate about their effect. The temptation to wrestle with the problem may be strong, but resist. Buying into another person's speculative scenario creates the impression that you are endorsing it, even though you understand that it is hypothetical.

* * * * * *

In dealing with hypothetical questions, above all, never accept the premise out of hand.

* * * * * *

Begin your response by verbally flagging the question as "a hypothetical" or "an 'if' question." You then have three options:

1. You can respectfully decline to speculate.
2. You may choose to answer, making *it absolutely clear that you are speculating.*
3. You can respond with a reality-based answer.

Whether you choose to provide an answer or merely indicate your unwillingness to speculate, make sure you have clearly identified the problem *to the audience,* so they don't think you are being arbitrarily unresponsive.

CASE STUDY: Reagan administration Defense Secretary Caspar Weinberger did a fine job of this in an interview following the U.S. bombing of Libya in 1986. Chris Wallace of NBC News asked, "If this does not deter Colonel Qaddafi and terrorism continues, what then?" Weinberger responded, "That gets us into hypotheticals, and you know I try not to deal with those."

Having flagged the hypothetical, Secretary Weinberger then used the opportunity to bridge to a selling point when he added, "But I think it will send an unmistakable signal, and I think it will go very far towards deterring future acts."

TIP: *If you are confronted with hypothetical questions on the witness stand (as in an administrative hearing), you can sometimes be forced to speculate. In such a case, be sure to qualify each answer ("This is speculation, of course, but if I must, I'd have to say . . ." or "In answer to your hypothetical question . . .") This makes for a clearer transcript and a minimum of ambiguities later on about what part of your testimony was asserted as fact and what was forced speculation (see our discussion of being a witness in Chapter 17).*

> **TIP:** *Hypothetical questions crop up frequently in job interviews. Here again, flagging the question type is a good tactic. It lets the interviewer know that you're listening and that you're careful. For example: "If you're a product manager for Brand X and your market share drops by two points, what would you do?" It's a fair answer to flag the if: "Well, you're asking me to speculate on a matter I don't believe will come to pass. However if that were to occur, let me state . . ."*

DIFFICULT QUESTIONERS

We identify four problem questioner "types" who crop up frequently:

- The Supporter
- The Detailer
- The Negator
- The Filibusterer

The key to understanding these questioners is to remember that in a sense they aren't really questioners at all. The problems arise from the fact that each type is functioning for the moment as a speaker. The speech may be a generous statement of appreciation, a criticism or grievance, or a self-serving rhetorical orgy.

* * * * * *

In dealing with troublesome personalities in the presentation situation, you must take control.

* * * * * *

While there are exceptions, in most presentations it is your privilege to set the agenda. Although you don't want to be rigid about it, it is up to you to keep to that agenda: your message.

Dealing firmly and politely with those who seek to usurp the floor helps present you as a confident and assertive person, lending conviction to your message indirectly.

* * * * * *

Bonus:
It is almost always possible to use even troublesome en-counters as opportunities to deliver additional selling points.

* * * * * *

Let's look at problem questioners one by one.

The Supporter

You may be surprised to find support listed as a problem. It is, but only in one sense. Because of our cultural notions of modesty, it is hard for most of us to accept praise, directly and wholeheartedly expressed. It makes us uncomfortable and we want to make the situation go away as quickly as possible. In a presentation, this tends to result in, at best, a hasty word of gratitude, at worst, a piece of embarrassed self-effacement.

If we are aware of the problem, however, we can use supportive comments to our advantage:

• Openly and sincerely thank the speaker for the kind words.
• Tell why the appreciation is gratifying. You strive to do good work and appreciation adds to the satisfaction.
• Then add a selling point, a further example of achievements you feel are praiseworthy: "Thanks for your kind words, John. We do try to be good corporate citizens, and it's nice to know that our efforts are appreciated. One of our latest projects in a related area is . . ."

TIP: *You won't always be able to add the selling point, but it's nice to be prepared. At several points in this book we have suggested that the presenter make up a note card listing points he or she wants to score in the Q & A. In this situation it is usually pretty easy to bridge to one of the points on your card.*

The Detailer (aka the Nitpicker)

This is the person who likes to quibble with facts and figures. A natural response to this provocation is to get into a debate. This is also the worst response. The point raised by the detailer is usually minor and often insignificant. If you pursue it too far you can completely lose the rest of your audience.

The problem here is the competing claims of one individual versus the whole group. Politeness requires that you spend time with the questioner, but if you spend too much time, you lose everybody else. Tactically, your main goal is to deal with the question as expeditiously as possible.

If you are sure of your facts and figures, stand by them. If there is legitimate room for disagreement, volunteer to see the person after the meeting and resolve the matter then: "George, I'm not 100 percent sure of those figures. Why don't you see me after we finish here. I'll get all the information from you and then get back with the answer. . . ."

* * * * * *

Be absolutely sure you follow through on any pledges to "get back" with information or contacts.

* * * * * *

You can certainly include others, and again, this is a good opportunity to bridge to one of the larger issues and deliver a selling point.

"Anyone else who is interested is welcome to join us. Now the *issue* that George raises here is one I can discuss. . . ." In this way you can deal with the question in a reasonably short time without getting bogged down in a lot of nitpicking. You come out looking good: friendly, courteous, tolerant, concerned, helpful.

The Negator
This is the questioner with a personal problem or a negative statement that is clearly not a question at all. In this case you are being cast more in the mold of arbitrator or ombudsman than as a source of information. You would like to be helpful, if possible; at the very least you would like to *appear* concerned. But you don't want to take up the entire audience's time with one person's problem, which may be only marginally relevant to your agenda. You need to respond, but not to get sidetracked and lose your audience.

The solution is to take the problem where it belongs: outside the bounds of your Q & A.

• First, be responsive, if possible, to the issue being raised, if only to validate or acknowledge it: "I just don't know what happened to your brother-in-law. . . ."

- Next, indicate your willingness to help — and the restrictions you are operating under in this situation: ". . . and we don't really have time to discuss it *here* as fully as I would like."
- Then, offer to put yourself at the person's disposal outside of presentation time: "See me after the meeting and I'll be glad to do what I can to clarify this for you."
- Finally, try to use the incident in a positive way by addressing an issue that encompasses the point or problem raised by the negator: "But I'd like to point out — on the broader issue of jobs in general — that for the past two and a half years we've been striving . . . ."

By expressing compassion and/or a willingness to help, you make a favorable impression. By offering to deal with the issue or problem outside of the presentation context, you regain control of the proceedings. By addressing the larger issue, you are able to make a selling point. This is turning a problem into an opportunity; getting to the point.

The Filibusterer

This is the most flagrant variety of "problem non-questioner": The person who launches into a rambling, run-on statement that may show early promise of becoming a question but never does. It's an aggravated form of thinking out loud. Since the statement is almost always negative or critical in tone and is without any explicit statement to come to grips with and address, it tends to make both you and the audience uncomfortable.

The source of the discomfort here is the issue of control. You have nothing concrete to respond to; the "questioner" has seized control of the proceedings. This makes you anxious, and *it has the same effect on your audience*. Like it or not, they look to you to take and maintain control — which is your primary task here.

A natural impulse would be to interrupt and challenge the filibusterer, asking, "Well, are you going to ask a question or not?" Unfortunately, appropriate as this may seem, it is likely to seem rude and confrontational; it is better to avoid this kind of impression.

If he or she gives you an opening you can jump in and regain control by "answering": "Well, Chris, if I understand what you're asking . . ."

If not, as is often the case, your only recourse is to use what we call the "relay race baton-pass" technique. After listening politely for a while — twenty-five to thirty seconds is quite sufficient — you figuratively reach out and grab the baton (i.e., the monologue) from the filibusterer and run with it.

1. Look directly at the person.
2. Address him or her by name, if you know it (which generally causes the speaker to pause for a second or two).
3. Pick up on a few key words, and then start talking.

Begin by literally echoing the speaker's last few words. Talk a little louder and more forcefully than your filibusterer, and as you do so, move your eye contact to another member of the audience. Keep talking as you bridge to the general issue. This assertive technique is quite effective, and the audience will appreciate your taking control.

There are a few additional personality types that cause problems specifically in the context of meetings. We cover these fully in Chapter 17.

A Final Note. You may feel that we're a little rabid about pushing you to get your selling points in at every opportunity. In reality, it's a rare individual who actually turns the Q & A to advantage. We asked a person in one workshop, "How did you do on the Q & A?" He said, "Well, I had my answers ready, but they didn't ask the right questions!" If you really want the Q & A to work for you, you have to be like the notorious "Boss" (William Marcy) Tweed, grand sachem of Tammany Hall, who said about his career, "I seen my opportunities and I took 'em."

QUICK REFERENCE SUMMARY

- Watch for the "A or B" dilemma: being forced to chose between presented alternatives. A third choice may be the right one.
- With multipart questions, answer the part of the question that lets your selling point come through. It's generally your choice if you want to go on to another part of the question.
- In internal presentations, especially to your boss, you may have to answer all parts of a question. In this case, tackle the toughest part first, then easier parts, and end on a positive note.
- "Flag" hypothetical questions: "You're asking me to speculate . . ." or "That's a hypothetical . . ."
- Be prepared to express pride in project or company in response to a Supporter's questions or remarks.
- In response to a Nitpicker, stick to your guns if the point is important; if it isn't, concede that the fact may be true and offer to talk with the person after the session.
- Be aware of Negators. Stay calm. Don't buy into the person's negative tone or words. Don't get caught in a fight.
- Offer to see a Negator, and any other interested parties, after the presentation to deal with the related issue.
- Once you know you've got a Filibusterer on your hands (thirty to forty seconds should be long enough to tell), intervene by using the person's name (if you know it), and expressing concern over issues being raised. If you don't know the person, "take back the floor" by echoing the Filibusterer's words and bridging to another point.

CHAPTER 12

How Do I Get to Carnegie Hall?

You'll probably recognize that question as the opening line of an old joke. The punch line is *"Practice!"* Which is what you need to do if you truly want to become an accomplished presenter. You've learned enough just by reading *Get to the Point* to improve, but if you really want to be good, you must practice. Practice alone, practice with family, with colleagues, or with professionals — but practice!

Here's a whole chapter filled with advice and techniques to help you practice efficiently and enjoyably and get the most out of your effort.

GENERAL PRACTICE CONCEPTS

We'd like to start by giving you some general maxims about practice; how to make the most effective use of your time.

Don't work on too much at once. Like playing the piano, giving a presentation requires us to integrate a number of complex processes into one seamless performance. Especially in the early stages of practice, avoid trying to do it all at once. Break things down into discrete components, mastering each separately before putting them together.

By concentrating on one factor at a time, you will master the process more quickly than if you try to "do it all."

Feel free to be free. Practice time is the time to take chances. We strongly encourage you to try everything; any zany idea that comes into your head. Later on, you'll have time to weed out things that don't work, but some of the things you discover this way will become invaluable components of your personal style.

* * * * * *

If you don't take chances in a training session, you'll never do it in "real life."

* * * * * *

For peak performance, make it tough. Once you've mastered the fundamentals, make practice harder than the real thing; you'll perform better. Call it the "on-deck" principle: The batter waiting in the "on-deck circle" swings a heavily weighted bat so that when he gets to the plate, the bat he swings at the oncoming pitch will feel light.

> CASE STUDY: Len Dykstra, one of Baseball's best players in the 1980s and 90s, credits his success to just this kind of approach: making the practice task harder than the real thing. Dykstra set out to learn to hit a major league fastball by batting against "Iron Mike," the pitching machine. He began at the normal distance — sixty feet, six inches from the pitching mound. Once he was comfortable hitting what the machine threw from this distance, he began to move closer to the machine, effectively reducing the time the eye and brain had to track the ball's trajectory and set the bat on a collision course. Eventually he got as close as forty-five feet to the Iron Mike and was hitting balls that were faster than anything a human being could possibly throw.

If you design your practice to be tougher than the real thing, you too can have that performance edge. If you know you have ten minutes to give your presentation, make sure you can do it in eight — without rushing. When you practice for your Q & A, really dig deep and look at every embarrassing, malicious, or underhanded question that your worst enemy might raise. Prepare for the toughest presenting slot: Assume that you're going to be the fourth of six speakers, so you'll find a way of launching your talk that will really wake up the audience.

Whatever practice devices you come up with, challenge yourself. The more closely you can approximate real presentation conditions, the more your practice will pay off.

Presentation Practice

Out loud, please. Most of the work we've done so far in *Get to the Point* has been in terms of the written word. Presentation making, however, is a spoken skill, and to master it you have to transfer your skills into the speaking mode.

＊ ＊ ＊ ＊ ＊ ＊

When you're actually making a presentation, your mind, your body, and your voice all have to work together. Therefore, they all need to be used in practice workouts.

＊ ＊ ＊ ＊ ＊ ＊

Thought patterns and sentence structures differ radically between writing and speaking. The average spoken sentence, for example, contains nine words; the average written sentence, twenty-three. What looks good on paper may sound unnatural and therefore unconvincing delivered vocally. Listeners tend to detect — even if only subconsciously — a "reading quality," which diminishes your overall credibility.

Perhaps the primary reason is that verbal speech dances to the rhythm of the breath; written speech has its own, quite different rhythms. Working from written text, you may find it hard to breathe properly. (This is one reason we encourage using notes rather than a full transcript.) So, to be effective, your practice must be done out loud.

> **TIP:** *Stretch physically and vocalize a bit before practicing in order to get into the habit before the real presentation. (See Chapter 13 for recommended exercises.)*

Get it on tape. By recording your practice sessions you increase their effectiveness immeasurably. The direct feedback of listening to your own voice, watching your own face and body is more valuable than a dozen critiques. In the early stages of practice, audio recording is fine; later on, you'll want to do videotaping, if at all possible.

> **TIP:** *With the accessibility and portability of cassette and micro-cassette recorders, you can make use of "dead" time like commuting time for presentation practice. In the privacy of your car you can both record and listen. On public transportation you may feel inhibited about speaking into your recorder, but with a tape player and headphones, you can certainly listen discreetly.*

Practice Plan

Divide and conquer. As we suggested above, practice pays off better if, instead of attacking the whole presentation at once, you divide it into brief segments and work on each segment separately.

A logical place to start would be with your opening, which you'll memorize. Practice the *whole process* of beginning your talk. If using a lectern, literally walk up to a lectern (a box on a table will do) and put down your notes. Pause. Visualize the room you'll be in and the people you'll be addressing; actually look at them in your mind's eye. Make mental eye contact, take three deep breaths, and launch into your grabber. Once you've finished, turn off the recording machine, rewind the tape, and listen.

Self-critique. Your first assignment on playback is to notice what you did well. This may not be easy. We humans tend to be hypercritical of our own performances, wincing at every little imperfection and remaining deaf and blind to our strengths.

* * * * * *

The key to effective self-criticism is detachment.

* * * * * *

Try to be like another person while you listen. This may be tough at first, but it makes a big difference in what you're able to hear.

So, from as objective a point of view as possible, what did you like about your performance? Was your voice animated? Did you sound confident? Conversational? Whatever it was that you felt good about, dwell on it awhile; feel that strength, let it sink in, reinforce it. Then move on to considering what needs improvement.

The "Rule of Three": Don't be afraid to do "retakes" as you practice your segments. Generally, it takes at least three tries to achieve a suitably polished, confident, and convincing rendition. However, if you feel additional run-throughs would strengthen your performance further, by all means do them.

Audio checklist. Go through the playback-self-critique process for each segment of your talk. Here's a list of things for you to listen for:

- Is your voice clear?
- Are your selling points strong and clear?
- Do you sound audience-centered?
- Did you use signal words to continually pull the audience in?
- Is there any phrase or image that might be developed as a theme throughout your talk?

Do you need to:

- Slow down?
- Speed up?
- Vary your pace?
- Did you take time to breathe?
- Did you pause occasionally?
- Was your voice flexible in pitch? Did it move up and down the musical scale, or did it hover within a limited pitch?
- Did you make effective use of emphasis, giving life to the emotional words, the action words?
- Are you unconsciously stressing the prepositions and/or conjunctions?
- Did you ever emphasize by lowering your voice?
- Did you keep phrases short and crisp, or did you ramble on and on and on, gasping for breath?

Record, play back, study, and rerecord each segment of your talk until you no longer find any major problems, until you've bolstered **all** your strengths to the maximum.

Once each segment is working smoothly, put them all together and practice the presentation as a whole. (If yours is a long presentation, you may want to assemble short segments into intermediate-sized sections before practicing the whole thing.)

Skill drills. In addition to working on your presentation section by section, you should devote some time to practicing specific skills. Listening to yourself and going through the vocal checklist should quickly reveal the areas that need work.

If you're a natural monotone, for example, practice — especially with feedback from your tape recorder — can change this. This is a situation where you really need to give yourself permission to take some chances — even to feel silly for a while, if necessary. Keep it firmly in mind that this is only practice; you've got nothing to lose but your inhibitions.

For working to change a monotone, choose a short selection of material as a practice piece. It could be from your presentation or it could be something else, but in either case it should have some excitement to it, some emotionality. Pick out the active words, then work on making them come alive. Try out different effects. Move the voice higher and lower — to the very top and bottom of your range. Exaggerate. Be outrageous. Explore your limits.

You'll soon find it doesn't sound so outrageous. You might even like your new vocal expressiveness. In any case, you can always tone it down when you're in front of an audience if you need to.

Another psychological technique to improve your vocal expressiveness is to imagine that you are giving your presentation over the radio — that your voice is the only tool you have to make your points. Treat your tape recorder like a broadcast microphone as you tape your practice session; then imagine it is a radio as you play back your tape. Would you tune in to hear this commentator again?

What you can hear on a tape if you're listening carefully is amazing. You should even be able to hear where you gestured. You can't hear the actual gesture, of course, but you can hear where your voice got animated. If that didn't happen very often, practice can help here, too. Find a private practice space and read or act out a practice piece, gesturing emphatically on the thoughts or ideas you want to stress. As with your previous vocal practice, really exaggerate and be expansive. Read newspapers, poetry, lines from a play, speaking faster and slower. Try for effective delivery at a variety of tempos.

If you rarely or never paused and were out of breath, you need to work on your phrasing. Again, working out loud with written material, your own or others', is the best regimen. Use a copy you can mark up. Divide the text into short, crisp phrases. Indicate your pauses and word stress, and phrase groupings in the manuscript with our script marking symbols (or invent your own):

/ for a brief pause; // for a longer pause

⌢ to tie groups together

∨ to indicate a breath

Mark on your notes anything you need to remember. Inflection, pace, pauses, and gestures can all be indicated on your note cards. It can be a symbol — like an upward or downward arrow to indicate pitch or a stick figure with arms upraised to remind you to gesture — or a word — "SLOW DOWN," "FASTER," "BREATHE," "SMILE," "EYES."

Don't worry that you shouldn't be looking at your notes often enough for this kind of reminder to help much. This is practice, remember? At this stage, look at your notes as much as you need to. As you practice, you will learn to do these things naturally. Any that remain stubborn can be marked in your final notes.

Listening is learning. Here's a supplementary assignment for you: Listen to others as you go through your day. Listen to the way people speak. Listen with real attention. Material is everywhere, and we suggest you concentrate on:

- Professional actors and announcers (television and radio news broadcasters, especially the better known ones, are good models)
- Nonprofessional communicators in informal circumstances; any conversation in which people are at ease and not self-conscious

Listen for all the elements of inflection, phrasing, and emphasis that we covered in Chapter 9. If you hear something you like, something that stimulates your listening attention, work it into your own delivery.

The video eye. Once you've worked through your presentation — segment by segment — and practiced all the skills you felt needed improvement, it's time to try to gain the use of a videotape system. Videotaping yourself is not indispensable; but it is quite valuable. Everything an audio recording can tell you about your verbal presentation, a video recording will tell you about your expression, gestures, and body language.

Set the camera up to record a full-length view of you. You don't want to be a talking head here, because that's not what people will see.

For rehearsal purposes you need to be able to observe your face and your upper body, particularly your arms and hands.

Video checklist. Tape your delivery. Play it back. As with the audio taping, your first assignment is to notice what you liked about it. Notice everything you did well. Then look for spots or aspects that need improvement.

- Was your face expressive?
- Or a frozen mask?
- Did you remember to smile?
- Before you began?
- From time to time during your talk?
- Was your body loose and mobile?
- Or did you stand like a wooden Indian?
- Were your gestures full and fluid?
- Or were your shoulders immobile?
- Or were your elbows frozen to your sides?

If you had a lot of trouble with one specific aspect of delivery — gestures, for example — tape your delivery several times, concentrating on that one skill. Keep taping it until the embarrassment — that feeling of "this can't be me doing this" — goes away.

As with your audio tape practice, record, play back, study, and re-record until you've eliminated all the problems and maximized your strengths. Plan to videotape your entire presentation two or three times.

Once your delivery is smooth, add your visuals. Actually observing the orchestration of your visuals on video can help tremendously in polishing this aspect of your presentation. The audience's point of view really lets you learn from experience how long a pause is needed to absorb each image. (It also reveals how good your visuals are. If they're too complicated or are poorly designed or laid out, you'll see it better on the video playback than you will looking at the visual itself. This is the time to make any improvements.)

Q & A practice. If your talk will include a question and answer session — or if it is an internal presentation in which you will be subject to questions, either at the end or throughout — you will need to do some Q & A practice. If at all possible, have other people help you out on this. If not possible, you can do quite a bit on your own. Refer to our

Q & A practice suggestions in Chapter 10. As you review your audio tapes and/or videotapes of Q & A practice, be alert for the following basics:

- Did you answer the question?
- Did you recognize tricky question forms?
- Did you clearly flag tricky questions when you recognized them?
- Did you bridge to a selling point?
- Did you shift your eye contact?

Critiques from others. Once you feel you have derived all the benefit you can from the direct feedback of practicing with recording devices, see if you can enlist a volunteer audience to view your presentation. If you have friends, colleagues, or mentors who are experienced in presentation techniques or public communication in general, solicit their advice and criticism. Even if you don't have experts at your disposal, invite anyone you can get to sit still long enough and listen — friends and family will usually help. If you can coax some candid comments from them, so much the better. Even without feedback at this point, just presenting in front of an audience will help make you that much more comfortable when the actual presentation time comes.

QUICK REFERENCE SUMMARY

- Divide your presentation into components to avoid frustration.
- Take chances; go beyond what is usual for you in voice, tone, pitch, and gestures.
- Breathing exercises will help calm your anxiety.
- Practice out loud. Use a tape recorder — video or audio.
- Stretch physically and vocalize a bit before practicing in order to get into the habit.
- If using a lectern for presentation, use a lectern (or some semblance) for practice. A box on a table will do.
- Listen and/or watch your tapes as if the taped performance were someone else's; be objective.
- Always note what is good before dwelling on what needs improvement.

- Retape segments again and again, trying variations in your voice — in sound level and enunciation.
- When you pinpoint areas to work on — pacing the voice, for example — devise exercises to correct the problem. Read newspapers, poetry, lines from a play; speak faster, slower, trying for effective delivery at a variety of tempos.
- Don't worry about referring to notes in practice; use them as much as you need to.
- Spend the bulk of your practice time working with audio tape. You can actually hear more — breathing, inflection, voice dropping at ends of sentences — than on video, since you aren't distracted by the visual element.
- Do plan to videotape your presentation at least two or three times if at all possible.
- Once comfortable with speaking, add your visuals.
- Remember to pause when you show a visual. Turn to the audience and talk.
- Remember to summarize after your talk — even in practice. Leave on a high note.

CHAPTER 13

Performance Anxiety: Dealing with Nerves and Tension

There's more to being a polished performer than mastery of technique. All the technique in the world won't guarantee a great presentation if you're so tense that your body conveys discomfort to a degree that overshadows your words. Indeed, nervousness and physical tension are the things people fear most about public speaking.

* * * * * *

Almost everybody experiences nervousness in front of a group or audience.

* * * * * *

This chapter deals with nerves and physical tension. And the bottom line is that both are natural and controllable.

Actress Helen Hayes, "First Lady of the American theater," was asked in an interview late in her career whether she still got nervous before a performance. "Sure," she replied, "I still get butterflies before every performance. But over the years, I've managed to teach them to fly in formation."

For some people nervousness is an affliction that goes away over time, or that disappears when they are making a lot of appearances — only to reappear when they haven't been in the spotlight for a while.

For others, in some degree it is always there. And this group includes quite a number of professional performers — like Helen Hayes.

Some nervousness is perfectly natural. There are two types of nervousness. "Fight or flight" most often stems from inadequate preparation. The other is a more positive anxiety, the kind a racehorse feels at the starting gate. It's a positive adrenalin flow. You should feel thoroughly prepared if you've followed the *Get to the Point* program, so we hope you won't experience the first type of nervousness. You really ought to have the second kind. If you don't feel an excited anxiousness at all, it means you really don't care. Even so, nerves are nerves. When your knees are shaking it doesn't matter what the source of the problem is. The objective here is to give you the tools to keep nervousness to a manageable minimum.

TEACH YOUR BUTTERFLIES TO FLY

If you understand that nerves are natural and can accept a certain amount of nervousness as normal, you are well on the way to getting it under control. Nervousness, like other forms of fear, feeds on itself. Without awareness, that little voice inside your head saying, "Look how nervous you are! What a terrible, inadequate person you are!" will go unchecked. This will put you at a real disadvantage.

Accepting your nervousness is the first step in reducing it. After you've done that there are a number of other measures you can take to keep it under control. Since nervousness is both a mental and a physical phenomenon — it originates in the mind but is expressed by the body — we need to address both the body and the mind to deal with it.

Psych-ups: The Mind

Your concepts, attitudes, and mental images are the sources of your nervousness. These are often unconscious, which makes them tricky to deal with.

The bugaboo of formality. If you simply start with the idea "speech" at the back of your mind, you're already in trouble. If you can intercept this thought and counter it by consciously picturing yourself in a conversational situation, you've won half the battle.

The fear of fear itself. Another problem is the fear that the audience will see your nervousness. This is actually two fears: one, that your listeners do perceive your feelings; and two, that they think badly of you for having them. Your unconscious mind thinks, "They know how nervous I am," and then, "They must think I'm terrible." You're likely to be wrong on both accounts.

The fact is, audiences are largely unaware of a speaker's nervousness. They've got lots of other things to pay attention to. Make yourself a big note in red at the top of your first note card: "I FEEL CONFIDENT!" It should help reduce your anguish. Another phrase that works is: "I'm glad to be here."

The other thing to keep in mind is that even if some of your nervousness does communicate itself, audiences tend to be forgiving, not judgmental. Evidence of your human fallibility will often evoke an empathetic response. Sounds unlikely? Look at your own experience as a member of an audience. Have you been to a presentation where the speaker really blew it? Just plain got lost and had to start over? What was the reaction? Usually it's forgiving and supportive. The typical listener's feeling is, "There but for the grace of God go I."

Keep in mind, though, that this isn't a free pass to blunder your way through a presentation. Especially in a business meeting setting, there's an impatient attitude lurking right behind the forgiving one. That audience sits through a lot of meetings and will be empathetic to a point, but they want to get something *useful* from each one.

Get the audience involved. Making the presentation interactive as soon as possible is another technique that helps many presenters get over their nerves. Interaction — give and take — is like conversation: familiar and comfortable.

One simple way to introduce an interactive element is to poll the gathering on some preselected questions; ask for a show of hands. A similar technique is to pose a specific question and field an answer. Be prepared to bridge to the right answer if you don't get the one you were looking for.

It might go something like this: "Given our present market position, who can suggest a merchandising scheme for our new self-adjusting widget?" One member of the team might suggest, "How about a drive-time radio contest?" You now bridge to your answer: "Well, Jack, I know how well that worked for the high-performance mini-widget, but what we've been looking at for SuperWidget III is a direct mail/store coupon offer."

Mental imaging. Many people — including a number of world-class athletes — use the powerful techniques we call mental imaging to combat nervousness and improve concentration. One imaging approach involves creating a strong mental picture of the result you want to achieve. This can be as simple as seeing yourself walking away from the lectern feeling great after a successful presentation. Or it might be more specific: the committee voting to accept your recommendation, for example. Whatever the desired outcome, bringing a positive mental image of it to the presentation should help make things go well.

A different approach to mental imaging is used by many speakers to overcome persistent "audiophobia." Sir Winston Churchill is reputed to have been petrified in front of an audience — until he hit on the idea of imagining his listeners sitting naked in the audience! He mentally turned the tables, "projecting" (in psychoanalytic jargon) onto his audience the sense of vulnerability he felt himself.

If you like Sir Winston's image, use it; we're sure he'd be delighted. If that one doesn't suit your personality, here are a couple that we have found useful: Instead of unconsciously wondering, "Will they like me?", reverse the positions; ask yourself, "I wonder if I will like them?" Or say to yourself as you approach the lectern, "Okay, now I'm going to do everything I can to make them comfortable." Be on the lookout for an image all your own; it will be the most effective of all.

Reminders, breaking the cycle. Since nervousness begins in the unconscious and automatically reinforces itself once begun, one of the practical problems in combating it is finding a way to break the cycle. As we suggest elsewhere, you can use your notes as an aid in refocusing your awareness. Write in an occasional reminder key. It could be as simple as "SMILE" or "BREATHE" or "MAKE THEM COMFORTABLE," written in big, easy-to-read letters. Notes like this can be a lifeline to grab when the nerves start to buzz. These techniques probably won't make your butterflies go away, but they should help you to keep them in formation.

The Body and The Voice

Nervousness usually manifests itself physically in the form of muscular tension. In order to give our bodies the best opportunity to perform well, we need to release as much of the tension as possible beforehand and then continue to channel it out of the body as we go along.

⍟ ⍟ ⍟ ⍟ ⍟ ⍟

*If circumstances permit, do a real physical warmup before
your talk — bending and stretching.*

⍟ ⍟ ⍟ ⍟ ⍟ ⍟

If tension is a particularly big problem for you, you might want to
do some fairly strenuous exercise. If you're a jogger, jog. If you play
racquetball and the facilities are available, do that. You can do this as
much as an hour or two beforehand and you'll still feel the beneficial
effects at presentation time.

Most of the time, of course, a major physical workout won't be possible. But if you have access to a reasonably private room before you
are scheduled to appear, you can do some of the less strenuous kinds of
warmups that singers use.

THE GET TO THE POINT *WARMUP PROGRAM*

The Body
For the following warmups, just before your presentation stand in a
comfortable position.

Fingers, wrists, and arms. Start by wriggling your fingers; then shake
your wrists; finally, the arms. You should feel all the joints loosening
up.

Shoulders. Stand tall, feet apart, as if you were supported by a string
attached to the very top of your head. Let your shoulders hang naturally. Then draw the shoulders up high; try to touch your ears. Hold
that position for a slow count of three. Then relax the shoulders and let
them hang again. Repeat this several times. A variation on this is the
"shoulder roll": First shift your shoulders forward as far as they will
comfortably go. Hold. Then move them up — and hold. Then all the
way back — and hold. Finally, press them down as far as they will
go — and hold. Reverse the direction if you wish. Repeat the cycle until
your shoulders feel loose.

Neck and surrounding muscles. Stand in a relaxed posture and gently
let your head drop forward. Feel the neck muscles stretch. Then, very
slowly, like an elephant swinging its trunk, roll your head sideways. To
give you an idea of how far, imagine a clock face: In the head-down

position you're at six o'clock; you want to roll your head up past nine o'clock, then counterclockwise to six and up past three o'clock. Continue this gentle rolling — stretching two or three times in each direction — or until all the kinks are out.

Warning:
Don't roll all the way around the back. This can hurt both the neck muscles and the larynx (what we usually call the "vocal chords," although there are no "chords").

The mind. Calm yourself before presentation time by listening to soft music. If you need to get psyched up, rock and roll or other more spirited music can be helpful.

The Voice
The jaw. Follow these steps:

- Loosen the lower jaw by moving it from side to side.
- Work the jaws in a chewing motion.
- Stretch your mouth W-I-D-E open. Feel the jaw and facial muscles loosen.

The lips. Relax the muscles in and around your lips by making the sound we make when we are cold. (We usually spell it "Brrrr," but it doesn't really sound like that.)

The voice. Start on a low pitch and softly hum. Let the voice move up and down as high and as low as you comfortably can. Remember, keep it *soft;* this is literally a stretching exercise for the larynx, and gentle is better than forceful. A minute or two of humming should leave your voice feeling clear and flexible.

The chest. Whether or not you had the opportunity to do any of the foregoing, always take a few deep, deliberate breaths just before you go on. The technique is straight out of self-hypnosis: Inhale slowly through the nose, letting your chest expand, filling your lungs to capacity. Hold the breath for a moment before exhaling slowly and quietly through the mouth.

This is a good basic set of loosening-up techniques. Of course, you may add others that work for you.

TIP: *Do not consume alcohol or caffeine just before a presentation. Alcohol can dull your senses. Caffeine can make you too jumpy.*

Once you begin speaking, you need to stay loosened up. And the best way to accomplish this is . . . yes, to *gesture*. Don't hang on to the lectern or clasp your hands. These positions not only prevent you from making gestures, they give the muscles something to tense against. And tense they will; it's almost like doing isometric body-building exercises. If you can keep your arms and upper body moving, however, you burn off your muscular tension.

QUICK REFERENCE SUMMARY

- It's natural to be nervous. Some natural anxiety helps your presentation.
- Channel tension out of your body through gestures.
- Calm yourself by breathing correctly and deeply.
- Prior to presentation time, if you need to calm down, try listening to soft music. If you need to get psyched up, listen to rock and roll or other more spirited music.
- Think of your presentation as a chat; this makes it less stiff.
- Make your presentation as interactive as possible. Ask questions of the audience early in the presentation or invite questions from the audience as you go along.
- Use mental imaging — see the process through to the end in a positive way.
- Use your note cards to remind yourself to "SMILE," "STAND STILL," "PAUSE," etc.
- If possible, do a real physical workout — running, swimming, racquetball — a couple of hours before presentation time to get your body loosened up.
- Do warmup/relaxation exercises on pages 159 and 160 or find your own way to get physically relaxed.
- Do not consume alcohol or caffeine just before a presentation.

14

Clothing:
What the Well-Dressed
Presenter Wears

Carefully and thoughtfully chosen, your clothing can lend powerful support to your physical presence. Generally this support should be unobtrusive, so you might save the sartorial spectaculars for the weekends and non-presentation days.

* * * * * *

You should dress well, but your clothing should not call attention to itself.

* * * * * *

Clothing that captures the audience's attention interferes with the message you want to deliver. Remember that you are there to make a statement, not your clothes.

* * * * * *

For virtually everyone, presentation dress means "business dress."

* * * * * *

With the advent of "casual days" and Silicon Valley dress codes, business dress has different meanings for different industries and companies. Don't let your clothes cost you any points or cause someone to miss your message.

For men, this means business suits (or shirtsleeves in some companies, if the meeting is around the conference table); for women, suits, dresses, or skirt-blouse ensembles. The exceptions to business dress would be uniforms for military personnel and possibly police or other uniformed public officials and perhaps a lab coat or hard hat for a scientist, engineer, technician, or plant manager giving a media interview in the workplace. *If your company or organization is casual, it's safe to err on the better dressed side of casual.*

We used to counsel conservatism in presentation dress: When in doubt, go for a more conservative look. Today we are happy to report a real trend away from the ultra-conservative dress mode in most industries. Without going too far out on a limb, we can say there is greater flexibility — a greater range of acceptable styles and modes today than in the recent past, particularly for women. The key factor is knowing your business and following the prevailing political dictates regarding clothing choice.

* * * * * *

Know your industry and your specific audience.

* * * * * *

Dress codes differ markedly from industry to industry, profession to profession. Bankers do not dress like entertainment industry executives. We trust that you are familiar with the traditions operating within your organization and your industry. You should also be aware that dress standards vary from region to region.

CASE STUDY: A New York City-based executive was called to testify at a regulatory hearing in a small New England town. He wore what he thought was appropriate clothing; what he was accustomed to wearing at such hearings in New York. This consisted of a dark blue pinstriped suit with vest, white shirt, and dark tie. As he walked into the hearing room, he overheard one of the commissioners whisper to a colleague, "The only time we dress like that in these parts is when we're carried out in a box."

Adjusting dress to conform to regional preferences is a complicated issue. It certainly isn't simply a question of "when in Rome, do as the Romans do." Your audience knows you're not a Roman, and pretending to pass yourself off as one may be seen as patronizing — you may thoroughly alienate your audience. A Yankee wearing new cowboy boots in El Paso is what we call an "easy mark."

The best counsel we can offer on this aspect of presentation dress is that you seek specific advice from someone in the place you will be making your presentation. Remember that this advice needs to take into account the image you wish to project and the nature of the proceedings as well as your regional identity.

If, for example, you're a financial officer from the Boston office going to handle a tax audit at corporate headquarters in Houston, find someone in Houston who can help you work out a dress approach that fits in, rather than calling attention to any aspect of regional identification. In other words, you may want to make some adjustments in your clothing.

QUALITY SHOWS

Although most of what follows has to do with specifics of style, color, patterns, and fabrics, something perhaps more important than these is the question of quality. With clothing, more than many things in this world, you get what you pay for. A superior quality suit communicates an image of confidence and authority to those you address. The fact that you will feel more confident and authoritative is an important reason for wearing fine clothes. We suggest that money spent on fine clothes for your presentation appearances is money well spent. Even if it seems extravagant at the time of purchase, it will pay off in overall presentation effectiveness.

Remember, your clothing can give you strong, unobtrusive support for your image and your message. Buy the strongest support you can find.

> **TIP:** *When you're making an important presentation, wear something that you like and that makes you feel good. If your clothes put you in a positive mood, chances are you'll make a more effective presentation.*

GUIDELINES FOR MEN

Suits

Fabric: Wear wool. Although we think of wool as winter wear, its properties really make it the fiber of choice for all seasons. Tropical-weight wools are nearly as cool as any other hot weather fabric, they tend to breathe better, and they unquestionably look better. Besides, rooms are air-conditioned in the summertime.

Colors: The darker tones — navy, gray, even black — can generally be worn in all seasons. The darker the shade, the greater the sense of formality and authority. The turn away from conservatism in dress is reflected in the fact that lighter colors are now a possibility in the summertime. A rich beige works especially well with a light blue shirt.

Patterns: Pinstripes, especially subtle ones, are acceptable in many industries and regions and virtually required in some. Save checks for the country club. If you are a professor, you may wear tweeds.

Vests: While vests were generally out of fashion at the time of this writing, they will come back in style at some point. So here are a few rules: Except on television where they add roughly fifteen pounds to your looks, vests look fine. But we recommend they be avoided because they tend to constrict your breathing. If you feel you must wear a vest, make sure it is loose enough for you to breathe easily and deeply. Also, if you wear a vest, it's fine to leave your jacket unbuttoned; if not, we recommend buttoning the jacket. In a seated presentation leave your jacket open.

Shirts

Fabric: Wear cotton or cotton blends.

Colors: Wear white, off-white, pastel, light grays, or neutrals. For television appearances, white shirts are generally out. Their brightness causes the cameras' automatic exposure control to overcompensate, resulting in underexposure of your face. If you are unable to consult wardrobe or other production people, stay on the safe side and wear a standard pastel — blue, yellow, or pink — or an off-white.

Patterns: Another area in which clothing conservatism has relaxed is shirt fabric patterns. At the time of writing, there are some very nice patterned shirts. Stripes are generally fine, especially the more traditional pinstripes. Avoid busy, loud patterns and strong colors.

Sleeves: Wear long sleeves for a finished look.

Details: Wear button-down or classic pointed collars. Trendy or unusual collar styles and other shirt details are out of place.

Ties

Fabric: Silk is best.

Patterns: Solids or simple patterns are best. Foulards, paisleys, and flowers are not recommended for presentations. One dress consultant recommends that you choose ties from one of the familiar categories that can be described in a single image such as solid, polka dot, "repp" (i.e., stripe), or club.

Color: The range of acceptable colors is wide. If in doubt, tone it down. Red ties — or ties with a strong red component — are very popular with television news broadcasters, not only because they show up well on camera, but also because the color reflects and adds flattering warmth to facial coloring.

Jewelry

Style: Avoid anything that calls attention to itself — unless you wish to refer to it. You might, for example, wish to wear a Kiwanis tie tack or a twenty-five-year service pin in your lapel. Gold watch fobs and other such adornments are best left at home.

> CASE STUDY: We once asked an executive whom we were preparing for testimony before a presidential commission in Washington, D.C., to remove his ID bracelet. We try not to overdo dress rules when working with clients, but in this case we were concerned that people would be distracted by this sparkler on his wrist rather than listening to his words. While ID bracelets were in vogue in his home state, in the hearing room in Washington the adornment was just in the way.

Shoes

Style: Any style of shoe you would normally wear to work should be fine for presentations. Any shoe that says "sport" should be avoided.

Principle:
Whatever style of shoes you choose, make sure they are polished.

Color: Black should be appropriate in any setting. Browns should be on the dark side. In some localities, brown shoes have negative connotations and should be avoided. If you are going to be presenting in an unfamiliar place, try to get an idea of the local attitude to brown — or settle for black.

GUIDELINES FOR WOMEN

As we suggested in our opening remarks, the what-to-wear question is considerably more open for women than for men. Women have gained sufficient acceptance in corporate culture that they can express their femininity a little more freely than was possible five or ten years ago. What we call the "deaconess" look — dark navy suit, white, high-collared blouse, and navy silk bow tie — is blessedly dead. Increasingly, women in executive positions are finding they can dress more in their own tastes without interfering with their career progress. We're happy to report that even in some very conservative areas (in certain investment banking companies, for example) it is a woman's ability, not her conformity to a strict, conservative dress code, that makes her promotable.

You know your working environment; suits may still be *de rigueur* in your industry. But even so, you may be able to cultivate little touches that lead away from the deaconess look. We feel you'll be more comfortable — more yourself — with your business (including presentation) wear, if you have a little fun with it. In fact, *too conservative* a look can be distracting in some businesses.

Suits

Fabrics: Wear wool, silk, and silk look-alike microfibers. One of a number of options that exist for women but not for men is knits. Suit, skirt, or dress, knits are perfectly acceptable presentation wear (subject to industry or regional exceptions). They offer the advantage of moving with your body more easily than in woven fabrics.

Make sure that they fit well and that the skirt lies smoothly over the hips.

Style: Designers are finally becoming more sensitive to the needs of working women and are making some stylish business-oriented suits, giving you a direction to move in — away from the prim, straightlaced look. There is also more of a spectrum now, so you can test the waters a little at a time.

Cut and fit: These are very important. A garment that really follows the contours of your body and moves with you when you move makes you look good. When you raise your arm to point at the screen, does the shoulder seam pull, the armhole bind? Can you button the jacket comfortably? (Actually, women don't need to keep suit jackets buttoned, but it's nice to have the option.)

Skirt length: Hem lines rise and hem lines fall. Even if miniskirts are in vogue for street wear, we suggest you consider knee-length or below the knee as standard for presentation dress.

Colors: There is a very broad palate of acceptable colors these days. It's easier for us to cover the unacceptables: Avoid anything distractingly bright, or overly patterned, garish, or loud. (Again, keep in mind the basic principle: You are the main attraction; your clothing is part of the supporting cast.)

Blouses

Fabrics: Wear cotton, silk, or fine synthetics.

Patterns and colors: Generally, keep them simple. Subtle stripes or other unobtrusive patterns are okay. Quite a range of color is possible, from traditional whites and pastels to vivid, jewel-like hues (best in silk and best under darker colored suits). Ruffled fronts are fine if not extreme.

Dresses

Fabrics: Wool (including knits), silk, or fine synthetics.

Patterns: Avoid busy patterns, extreme styles, plunging necklines, and anything that will actively distract from your presentation.

Hose

Wear neutral to dark tones. Subtle textures and patterns may work, depending on your business.

Shoes

Avoid boots, open toes, and sling-backs. By all means choose colors to coordinate with your outfit. Black patent leather or suede look good in all seasons. Even if you normally wear flats, we suggest you wear at least a little heel for presentations.

Hair

Careful grooming, not length or cut, is the issue. Keep your hair pulled away from your face. Nothing is more distracting than watching a woman constantly flicking hair out her eyes or not being able to see the eyes because of all the hair.

Jewelry

Jewelry should complement your clothing, not compete with it. Fashion trends come and go. So if it's currently fashionable to wear dangle or drop earrings, keep them conservative and not too distracting. Leave your diamonds and other sparklers at home. Pearls or other matte-finish pieces that don't reflect too much light are best.

Makeup

Every woman over the age of twenty-five should wear at least a little makeup for presentations; a little blush, mascara, and light lipstick. For presentations where you will be brightly lit — which includes television appearances — makeup will need to be heavier than your usual to create the same effect. Bright lights wash out skin tones.

QUICK REFERENCE SUMMARY

- Be aware of dress standards in your region and in your business or industry.
- While business dress standards are less conservative than they used to be (especially for women), avoid flamboyance.
- When in doubt, keep it simple and comfortable.
- Your choice of clothing can enhance your image as a presenter, making your message stronger.
- You should dress well, but your clothing should not call attention to itself.

CHAPTER **15**

Some Final Practicalities: Interruptions and Choreography

A few practical presentation matters that are not directly connected to any of the larger conceptual areas we have dealt with do nevertheless need to be covered. The two broad areas are the problem of interruptions and the choreography of microphones and the lectern.

INTERRUPTIONS

Interruptions can come from a number of sources. Someone may bring you a message; a person may wander into the meeting room by mistake; some members of the audience may carry on their own loud conversation; a truck driver outside may lean on his horn. The list is as long as the possibilities life brings. And you can be sure that some interruption or other distraction will plague your presentations from time to time.

Minor distractions — people occasionally walking in or out, a minor cough, a message handed to someone in the room — are fairly normal occurrences in meetings and presentations and can generally be taken in stride. After all, the show doesn't stop when one person arrives late to the theater. But major disturbances do call for action. The criterion for deciding whether or not to take action is *the degree to which it is likely to capture the attention of the listeners and interrupt communication.*

❋ ❋ ❋ ❋ ❋ ❋

If you try to compete with a distraction, you invariably lose.

❋ ❋ ❋ ❋ ❋ ❋

Acknowledge major interruptions immediately. Because no communication is going to take place, you might as well stop talking the very second you become aware that "something is going on." And that is precisely what you *ought* to do.

It's very simple. Stop speaking and wait for external or nonhuman distractions to pass. The dogfight outside the window will eventually wind down; the truck driver will stop honking; the airplane noise will die away enough to allow you to continue.

With human disruptions, however, your listeners will expect you to take control. If thoughtless colleagues are holding a private conversation, for example, generally all you need to do is stop and look over at them. The silence will most likely get their attention, and your eye contact will clearly communicate your feelings about the interruption.

Occasionally, this tactic will fail to work. Then you will have to take appropriate action to regain control of the proceedings. If it is a case of rudeness or insensitivity — people are talking and don't pick up your polite signals or simply won't shut up — you may have to say something. Responses vary with the person interrupting, so the specific approach you take is a judgment call. Let's consider some possibilities.

If an aide walks in with a note for a member of a meeting — let it go. If they engage in extended conversation, a pause would be appropriate. If the people interrupting are your equals in rank, you might ask them to keep it down or even to go outside the room to finish their conversation. If the disruption involves people senior to you, try extended silence. If that doesn't work, you might *politely* ask if they want you to wait until they complete their discussion. Sometimes well-meaning people are unaware of the disruptive effect they are having on a group.

If your disruption is a natural disaster — a member of the audience having a coughing fit, for example — try to alleviate the problem by handing the afflicted person a glass of water or some similar action. In such a case it is a good idea to offer an expression of concern, whether or not you actively intervene. A simple "Are you all right over there?" or "Do you think you'll be okay now?" will suffice.

TIP: *Any time someone delivers a note to you while you are presenting, you need to give the audience some indication of the contents or they'll wonder what it was about — and not pay attention to what you're saying. If it's for you, say so. If it concerns someone else in the room, pass on the message: "For the person who drives a blue Buick with Colorado plates: You left your lights on"; or "Sarah, you just received an urgent phone call. Go ahead; we'll fill you in on anything you miss."*

CHOREOGRAPHY

Like a ballet, a presentation contains movements — usually interaction with the physical setup — that need to flow smoothly if the performance is to be successful. We covered one such area, the choreography of visuals, in the context of our general discussion of that subject. Here we cover the other major areas of choreographic concern, relating to microphones and lecterns.

Microphones. Generally, if a meeting room or auditorium is large enough to require a sound system, it will have one. From the speaker's point of view, one sound system is pretty much like another, except for microphones. There are three types commonly in use:

- Fixed
- Wireless
- Clip-on

A fixed or "gooseneck" mic that's attached to the lectern attaches you to the lectern as well.

* * * * * *

If you have a choice, always request a non-fixed microphone, one that attaches to you.

* * * * * *

The wireless microphone, technologically the most up-to-date, is actually a tiny radio transmitter that sends your voice to the amplification system without any wires to encumber you. This gives you worry-free mobility — and makes the wireless mic your first choice. To "mic up," just clip the unit to your lapel, shirt, blouse, or necktie, about one hand's span (six inches) from your mouth.

Since wireless systems are relatively expensive, however, not every hall is so equipped. Midway between the fixed mic and the wireless, in terms of convenience, is the "clip-on" or lavaliere. This is a very small pickup that either hangs around your neck or fastens to your clothing with an alligator clip, like the wireless.

The clip-on gives you almost as much mobility as the wireless, but there is a cord to contend with — which adds one important step to the process of "micing up." First, attach or hang the mic about six inches from your mouth, as with the wireless. Then, to keep the wire out of the way of your hands and feet, lead it inside your jacket (if you're wearing one) and around to the back. Tuck a loop into the waistband of your skirt or trousers, making sure to leave some slack, and (for men) rebutton your jacket.

> **TIP:** *Women who wear dresses can tuck the mic wire into a belt or sash. If your dress is beltless, you'll have to do without this safety net.*

Aside from getting the wire out of the way, both physically and visually, this procedure gives you a safety net: If you walk away from the lectern without removing the mic — and it is easy to forget about these tiny mics — what happens? The mic crashes to the floor, sending an amplified thunderclap through the room. If you've tucked the cord into your waistband, then rather than jerking the microphone off your lapel, your motion simply pulls out the loop of cord and disaster is averted.

Lecterns. Inexperienced presenters often use a lectern as a crutch. Or perhaps "security blanket" is a better way to put it. The lectern provides the thing a drowning person desperately longs for: something to hold on to. But this proves to be a liability as well as an asset. The same mentality that craves something to hold on to won't let it go. This results in some postures you probably recognize: the "white-knuckler," who seems quite literally to be "hanging on for dear life"; the "ship captain," who leans in and grasps the lectern in a bear hug, listing first to one side, then to the other as he steers his ship through the perilous waters of his presentation. They may feel safer for their physical contact with the lectern, but they sacrifice their ability to move and gesture. The security blanket becomes a straightjacket.

Another reason to avoid grabbing or clinging to the lectern is that it tends to diminish your energy and results in shortness of breath and muscle tension. Gesturing will relieve the tension and help your breath supply.

Some presenters avoid the trap of physically grasping the lectern but instead use it as a sort of psychic shield or fortress, something to hide behind. Unseasoned presenters tend to stay firmly rooted behind the lectern, in effect imprisoned in their fortress. Others — we call them the "space walkers" — are able to get out from behind and drift a short distance, but they can get no farther away than the length of their arm, which acts like the hose that connects them to their life support system.

The lectern as psychic shield or fortress protects you, but conversely it acts as a barrier between you and your audience. Without the obstruction of a lectern, you simply have more presence; you're communicating more directly.

* * * * *

To the extent that you can free yourself from the lectern, your presentation stands to gain in liveliness and credibility.

* * * * *

Learn to move away from the lectern. Think of it as a place to park your note cards: Walk out from behind it as you develop a point; then, when you need to refer to your notes, simply walk back. If eventually you can do without the lectern altogether, so much the better. Presenting without a lectern doesn't fall under the heading of cardinal rules, but it's one of those subtle but significant factors that add up to making points.

QUICK REFERENCE SUMMARY

- Ignore minor distractions — someone walking into the room, a cough or sneeze. If a distraction affects audience attention, pause until it passes.
- If you try to compete with major disruptions in a presentation setting, you'll lose.
- Step one in responding to major interruptions or disruptions is to *stop speaking.* If the disturbance is human, look at talkers in silence. If not, simply wait for it to abate.
- If people are talking and don't respond to your silence, ask them to "keep it down" or finish their conversation outside.
- For coughing, sneezing, or choking fits, offer assistance, if possible, and make sure the person is okay.
- How long to wait during an interruption is a judgment call. Go with your experience and feelings.
- Listeners expect you to manage the group. Take action when necessary.
- If you receive a message when presenting, always let your audience know if it is for you. If it isn't, pass it along to whomever it is for.
- If your voice is to be amplified, choose a clip-on or wireless mic to give you mobility.
- Clip the mic one hand-span from your mouth and tuck the cord, if there is one, behind you in your belt or waistband.
- If you need to cough or clear your throat while wearing a mic, turn your head away from the mic.
- Don't lean on the lectern. It diminishes breath supply.
- Don't cling to the lectern; it creates muscular tension and prevents you from gesturing.
- A lectern is a barrier. The more you can get out from behind it and face your listeners, the more "presence" and impact your presentation will have.

CHAPTER 16

Media Interviews

We have prepared people for *60 Minutes, 20/20, MacNeil/Lehrer, Business Week, Good Morning America, The Today Show, Communications Week, Health Magazine,* and *Live at Five,* as well as for numerous live radio call-in shows, trade and consumer magazines and newspapers. So we know media interviews. We can tell you that, with the exception of the brief, spontaneous hallway, breaking news or "deadline" interview, ninety-five times out of a hundred media interviews provide an excellent opportunity to make your points — and usually to a very large audience.

Essentially, a media interview is a *presentation* in question-and-answer format. Like any Q & A session, you *do* have to answer questions put to you, but you can almost always get around to making — and emphasizing — the points you want to leave with the audience. All the basic presentation skills come into play in the interview, including writing or content-organizing, but most especially the question-preparation and bridging skills.

> **TIP:** *We have found that this one single concept: Thinking of your media interviews as a type of presentation makes all the difference in your ability to communicate the points you want to readers, viewers and listeners.*

* * * * * *

A reporter wants to hear your selling points; you're the "source," the expert, the person who can make him or her look good.

* * * * * *

Most of the time a reporter calls you because you have information he or she *needs* for a story. You are a Subject Matter Expert. The caveat of media interviews is that if you are not the expert, don't fake it. Your obligation is to refer the reporter to whoever is the expert. Learn the ways that we will presently describe to gracefully say, "I don't know" or "I'm not the expert in that subject . . ." and give them a source who can help them.

CASE STUDY: A CommCore consultant sat in an airplane seat next to an editor from a leading national newspaper. After the "what do you do" pleasantries, we mentioned that many of our clients complain that after an interview they are either misquoted, or the *wrong* quote is used.

The editor said, "I *never* intentionally misquote anyone. Which quote I use, however, is much more the responsibility of the person I interview than it is for the reporter.

"You see, when reporters ask questions, they take a lot of notes. I also use a tape recorder, but rarely have time to listen to it. At some point, I hit a deadline, when it's time to write. This could be the same day, or a week later. I first go back through my notes to find out what *I* think is important.

"This is too late for the spokesperson. Spokespeople should come into an interview with a clear idea of what their key points are. They also have the right to tell me what their key points are. They can say, 'What's important here . . .' 'This is a critical point . . .' 'Something that hasn't come up in other articles yet . . .'"

The editor continued, "If spokespersons would take the time to prepare and plan, I would be able to write my articles better and faster, and they would be more pleased with the quotes that I use."

Taking the time to prepare won't keep a good reporter from finding information from your competitors and detractors, but at least your side will be well represented.

BEFORE THE INTERVIEW

When the reporter calls, step one is to get his or her name and affiliation (paper, magazine, broadcast show) and ask, "Have you spoken to public relations?" That's the rule in most companies. In fact, several of our clients have a rule printed on their daily news summaries: "If you get a call from a reporter, or you have a newsworthy story, call _____ in media relations, at _____-_____." The public relations people will generally determine if you are the proper person to be talking to this reporter.

Ground rules. Once an interview has been set, the first thing to do is gain control by setting some ground rules. The most crucial thing to establish is the topic or purpose of the interview. Open-ended interviews have a way of getting out of hand. If for any reason you don't feel comfortable dealing with the topic the reporter is pursuing (or, as we mentioned, if you're not the expert), don't agree to do the interview. If you have no problem with the topic, you can proceed — and don't hesitate to keep the interview confined to the agreed subject. Be sure to find out when the interview will appear (print or broadcast).

If the interview has not been set up by the public relations department, you may wish to set other criteria or ground rules, such as arranging the date and time and/or location to suit your convenience, establishing a time limit for the interview, or imposing certain restrictions on subject matter. The latter will avoid "no comment" situations.

Audience profile. Your next step is to do an audience profile. Remember that the reporter is just a vehicle. Ultimately, your communication is not with the reporter but with the reporter's audience — the reader, listener, or viewer. The reporter, however, is your *means* of reaching your audience; in this case, the only means. So, read the paper; watch the show; find other articles by this reporter. See what kinds of approaches and quotes he or she tends to showcase. Also find out all you can about the demographics of the media's audience; call their ad sales department. All of this will prepare you to make the most of the interview opportunity.

Complete your interview worksheet. Before every media interview we recommend that you write down notes for yourself. Except for television interviews, where it looks too rehearsed, it's okay to have notes. We have created specific interview sheets for print, radio, TV and satellite interviews. Here are the basic categories.

INTERVIEW WORKSHEET

1. Background/overview.

2. What are your Selling/Message/Copy Points?

3. Minus/Plus Analysis.

4. Last Question Response.

5. Offer to Provide Additional Information.

Here's how we use the sheet.

1. **Background/overview.** This is where your research and preparation comes in. Besides knowing the subject, you should always find out where you are in the interview process. You are usually one of several people being interviewed for the article. So you need to think about what the others would say and how your quotes will survive the editing process.

    This category is also important in case the reporter starts with a narrow or nitpicky first question. You have the right to say: "Before I answer that question, let me put the issue into perspective . . ." Don't forget to answer the question; but you're allowed to put the answer in context.

2. **What are your Selling/Message/Copy Points.** These are your key messages that you need to communicate. See Chapter 4 on Building Strong Messages. In addition to answering the reporter's questions of Who, What, Why, When, Where and How, you should try to answer reader/listener/viewer responses: So What, Who Cares, What's In It For Me ("WIIFM")? Anecdotes, examples, case studies; i.e., what *differentiates* your organization, company, service or product.

3. **Minus/Plus Analysis.** This is where you write down all the questions you can anticipate and as well as your **Bridges** for going from the difficult questions to more positive information. Also in this category are the Types of Questions that we wrote about in Chapter 11.

4. **Last Question Response.** This is the favorite question of good reporters. They want to know if you have additional information that they didn't ask about or may have missed. As a spokesperson, you have only two good choices. Either repeat information that you have already communicated, or go down your list of message points that you wanted to talk about, and bring them up now. If the reporter forgets to ask you if you have anything else to communicate, you have the right to bring up *your* points here. Remember, some reporters are either not well versed enough in your subject, or perhaps too jaded, to ask for what *you* believe to be important.

5. **Offer to Provide Additional Information.** Often reporters need to do additional fact checking or to compare your statements with other spokespersons. If you offer to be available for follow-up, you increase your odds of being quoted favorably. If your public relations department has helped in the interview, it's usually proper to refer follow-up calls first to PR; they will track you down if the information requested is more than fact checking.

DURING THE INTERVIEW

Following are the most important rules to be aware of during interview time.

Remember the "Rule of Three." In a media interview, as much as any presentation, repetition is important. Instead of being encyclopedic about your subject, pick a few key points — usually three — and try to communicate them two or three times during the interview. Remember, the goal is to have your information in the article, and usually ahead of your competitors. While a reporter may find opposing information, repetition of a key point will usually result in your side being quoted.

In fact, we've reduced Rule of Three into a **Media Interview Equation: $3 \times 3 = 1$; $9 \times 1 = 0$.** This is not new math. The rule goes that if you have three points to get in and you mention them three times, it's almost a guarantee that at least one, perhaps two, will be written about or quoted in a story. If you have nine points, and manage to score all of them one time each, there's no guarantee the reporter will use any of those points. In fact, the reporter might use your point four, when you would have preferred a mention of number seven.

Be alert for "difficult" questions. Review the question types we covered in Chapter 11: the hypothetical, the false choice, the multipart, and the loaded question. Reporters wield questions all day long — this is their stock in trade — so they are masters of all of these.

> **CASE STUDY:** Be on the alert for confused, uninformed, or general questions that are an invitation for you to explain more of your material. Sometimes these are outrageous, as on one occasion when a New York area computer company executive was being interviewed by a reporter from a trade journal and was asked in the middle of the interview, "Excuse me, is this hardware or software we're talking about?" The point is that you, like the executive in the story, should be mindful of the opportunity, not the inappropriateness of the question. Use such questions as occasions to explain or even teach.

Flag your selling points. You know what your selling points are, but neither the reporter nor the reporter's audience does. Underscoring the points you consider vital with phrases like, "What's important here is . . ." or "I'd like to stress the following . . ." or "Something I haven't seen in other articles about this subject . . ." helps focus the audience's attention.

Never go "off the record." A reporter's job is to gather — and publish or broadcast information. If you don't want the public to be privy to it, keep it to yourself. "Not-for-attribution" comments are tricky stuff; we suggest you steer clear.

Never say "No comment." This doesn't mean you have to answer every question thrown at you in an interview, but it does mean you have to learn to decline gracefully. *"No comment"* has a combative, confrontational tone to it. It brings to mind television coverage of events like a drug bust where the suspect shields his face from the camera with his coat. You create a much more positive impression when you offer an explanation of *why* you decline to answer a question.

There are three areas of questioning that clearly violate the bounds of the "interview compact": questions that fall outside of the agreed topic, personal questions, and questions relating to proprietary information. You can set firm limits and still appear fully cooperative if you cover your refusal with a clear explanation. This works particularly well if you then bridge to related information you *are* prepared to discuss. For example, "That's really outside the bounds of what we agreed to talk about, but here's what I *can* say about the general issue you raise . . ."; "The FCC hasn't ruled on our petition, but I can tell you what we argued . . ."; "It's a matter under litigation and we can't talk about it until the courts have ruled. But our position is . . ." or "I'm sure our competitors would *love* to have that information, but we won't discuss this until we make our formal announcement. But if you'd like some general information . . ." "I'm not the expert in that area. What's your deadline? I'll make sure that someone gets back to you before then . . ."

End the interview after a reasonable length of time. Presumably, if you set a time limit you will adhere to it unless the interview is going very well and you think you can make a few more points by continuing. If it's going the other way, by all means terminate it after a decent interval.

Facilitate follow-ups. Let the reporter know where and when you can be reached for follow-ups and make yourself available as promised. Having taken the time to talk to a reporter, take the extra time to give him or her the opportunity to call you so that if there are questions, the information will be right when it's printed or broadcast.

SPECIAL RULES FOR DIFFERENT SETTINGS

Prearranged interviews. In cases where you know about the interview in advance, you can prepare fully. Find out both the topic and the format. You can research the general topic, which will give you an overall perspective, much as gathering an audience profile adds to your perspective in a standard presentation. This can guide you in preparing solid, well-developed selling points focused on the subject matter, with strong headlines and vivid supporting specifics.

Always be prepared to summarize your most important points. Remember, repetition builds retention. If a reporter hears one of your points three or four times, the chances are three or four times as great that it will be broadcast or turn up in print. Feel free to bring notes or a summary card just to make sure you don't forget any key points. For radio and print interviews — and certainly for interviews held over the phone — you should refer to your notes at any time. For on-camera interviews, you might carry a file card and refer to it discreetly from time to time — only during commercial breaks and only if you're a skilled spokesperson.

It is also a good idea to send background information to the reporter. The worst that can happen is that he or she doesn't read it. If the first question doesn't lead to a general statement of the background information, you can take a moment to provide it to the audience: "Well, Clare, I can give you those numbers in a moment. However, let me first take a little time to give you an idea of what this product means to us — its features and how we've positioned it . . ."

If appropriate, have props — products or books, for example — on hand to demonstrate one or more aspects of what you're discussing. If you're doing the interview at the studio, tell them in advance you're bringing something to show; they will then set up the best shot for viewing it.

Spontaneous on-camera interviews. These can be quite intimidating. After establishing the basics — primarily credentials and topic, as discussed above — ask for a few minutes to compose your thoughts. You should use this time to pull together a hasty but coherent agenda. Jot down your bottom line and your two or three main selling points if you can. You may or may not get a chance to refer to them, but even if you don't, writing them down helps fix them in your memory.

In addition to basic ground rules discussed above, get as comfortable as possible in a difficult situation: Ask that cameras, lights, and microphones be kept at a reasonable distance. To give yourself the same lifeline the reporter would take, ask for a retake on any fumbled answer. You may not get it, but generally reporters want you to look and sound good, so they might allow you to do a retake.

Interviews in your office. The main advantage to holding an interview on your own territory is that you will at least feel at home with the surroundings. Make the physical environment as pleasant as possible — get out from behind your desk and into a living room setting. All of this tends to diminish the natural atmosphere of tension.

Two other steps we suggest you consider taking are to invite your public relations representative to be present (if you have one) and to arrange to make your own tape of the interview. The former will help keep you and the reporter on track; the latter will serve as a "file copy" of the entire interview — not just the reporter's edited version.

TELEVISION APPEARANCES

Aside from straight reporting, which is covered in spontaneous on-camera interviews, virtually all television appearances for presenters fall into the broad category of news and information programs and talk shows. Appearing on television can be nerve-racking, but most people feel it's worth whatever discomfort it entails because it's great exposure. You really can't buy the kind of coverage you get for free from a guest appearance on television — the "third-party endorsement effect" — even with a no-expense-spared advertising budget.

To make your television appearance go as smoothly as your presentations, follow the basic training precepts we've discussed throughout this book: Get to know the show, host, and format — preferably by watching. Prepare a list of strongly delineated selling points. Arm yourself for difficult questions. Make a Minus/Plus sheet to guide you in bridging answers. Find out if there is a topic or theme; if so, slant your selling points and plan your bridges accordingly. Find out who else will be on the show; consider what topics and directions are likely to result. Plan bridges as appropriate.

If you plan to use props — a good idea to illustrate your points — or to give a toll-free phone number for further information, be sure to mention it to the producer prior to your studio appearance.

Dress. The first principle really goes without saying: Look your best. For the rest, our basic presentation dress principle applies: Your clothes should not call attention to themselves. It's you, not your wardrobe that people are interested in. White shirts cause photographic exposure problems with television cameras; they're too bright. Avoid this problem by wearing soft off-white or pastel colors. Ties or blouses containing some red reflect a flattering warmth to facial tones.

Arrival. Get to the studio well ahead of the scheduled time. Introduce yourself to the producer, makeup and wardrobe people, and, if possible, to the host. Don't be intrusive, but if you have an opportunity to chat with the host or anyone who helps determine content, use it. The more you can get across about yourself and your topic before things get under way, the more likely the interview will go smoothly and be interesting.

Even if you don't get a chance to speak with the show host beforehand, you can use the "mic check" — the part of the pre-show set-up where your microphone level is balanced with that of the host — to get a little information across. When the sound person asks you to speak into the microphone so they can get an accurate level, instead of following the traditional "Testing, testing; one, two, three, four," we suggest you simply identify yourself and your company or other affiliation and mention one of the points you'd like to make during the show.

This may seem ridiculous, but think about it. First, these are busy people who don't get a chance to do all the preparation they'd like. Second, they want the same thing you do: to get an interesting interview. Third, indicating that there are certain things you want to talk about is an immediate stimulus to the host to follow up on those points. The more of a sense the interviewer has of the areas in which you are interested and able to speak to, the greater the likelihood that the interaction will be entertaining — which means viewers will be less likely to flip the channel.

On camera. All the impression factors are doubly important on television. Here are some vital tips that should help make your appearance a success:

- *Posture.* You will generally be seated for most of your time on-camera. Sit forward in your chair and sit up straight. You don't have to sit literally on the edge of your seat, but definitely avoid lounging. Important: Lean in toward the host when you answer. This demonstrates energy and conviction.
- *Eye contact.* Maintain eye contact with the host even when the host looks at the camera. Don't worry about the cameras. You communicate to the audience through the host. In fact, keep your eye contact and posture until you hear an "All clear" or "We're off the air" signal so you don't drop your on-camera demeanor prematurely.

- *Smile.* Even when the show is on a sensitive issue, smile when you are introduced and when the show — or your segment — ends.
- *Gesture.* Keep your hands resting lightly on your thighs or on the table top. From these positions, it is easy and natural to gesture.
- *Be concise.* Try to keep your answers between twenty and thirty seconds.
- *Be dramatic.* Use visual images and analogies to help dramatize your points for the audience.
- *Offer tips,* if appropriate. The American public loves tips, and if they believe they have learned something useful from you, they may in fact remember your product, service, or message better.
- *Don't lose sight of your audience.* Never forget that you're really talking to the show's listeners, not the host or other guests. *Enjoy yourself!*

PRINT INTERVIEWS

In our media training seminars we usually introduce the print interview module with the statement: "The *good news* about print interviews is that they tend to go longer than broadcast, go into more depth and offer more time to know the reporter. The *bad news* is that print interviews tend to go longer than broadcast, go into more depth and offer more time to know the reporter."

What makes print an advantage can also be a pitfall. Yet, if you are prepared and think of print interviews as a presentation, you are bound to do well.

Print interviews lend themselves to signal words, putting issues in context and effective use of visualizations, anecdotes, and analogies.

Even more than for TV and radio, spokespersons should prepare the Minus/Plus analysis or Mind Map for the interview and stick to the agreed upon subject. Since print deadlines are often longer than radio and TV, always offer to provide additional information to the reporter or be available for follow up questions.

SATELLITE INTERVIEWS

Once the exclusive domain of *Nightline* and other national broadcasts, the satellite interview is now part of local news coverage and "satellite media tours." The rules for satellite media interviews also work for videoconferencing.

In addition to your basic preparation, you need to get comfortable with the technology — first the ear piece, also known as the "IFB," and second, the ability to get used to looking at the camera lens.

Before the satellite interview, learn what market or city you will be broadcast to. Try to localize your comments to that city. It's also a good idea to use the reporter's name; this also makes the interview seem as if you are in the local market.

It's important to arrive at the studio early enough to get comfortable with the physical layout. In some settings, you'll be in a chair, in others you might be on a stool.

Because this is a television interview, the producers may put a little make-up on you and mic you as they would for a normal television interview.

A technician will put the ear piece, IFB, in your ear and try to make it invisible to the viewing public. You have to make sure it's comfortable and you can hear. Take the time to make it as comfortable as possible and make sure the sound is clear.

For each market there will be a mic check. Take advantage of the mic check with by stating your name, organization or association and one point you want to get across.

Each interview must be fresh for the station. Most satellite interviews are edited, but an occasional one is live. Know in advance which are live or taped. Taped interviews offer a little more flexibility and allow retakes on questions that you can improve on. Even on a live interview, you can correct yourself to make sure you are being accurate.

Satellite interviews do have definite time limits, usually no more than 10 minutes per station. Take advantage of the last question response. Either the reporter will state, "This is the last question . . ." or you will hear, "We're running out of time . . ." In either case, be ready. If the question is one that you want to talk about, by all means, answer it. If it's one that you would rather not talk about, or you have an item on your agenda that you have yet to discuss, you can bridge to your point, by saying, "If we're running out of time, here's one point that I would like to discuss. . . ."

RADIO INTERVIEWS

Radio provides a terrific opportunity to reach key audiences. And given the proliferation of talk shows and drive time programs, radio stations are actually seeking spokespersons on many subjects. Since you can't be seen by the audience, it's even more important that you use your voice to impart enthusiasm and conviction to your comments. One of the ways to push that voice — although the audience will never know what you're doing — is to gesture when you answer questions. Gesturing (as discussed in Chapter 9) lubricates the voice, adds energy to your comments and burns off the normal tension that goes along with a media interview.

Radio interviews allow you to bring notes and props. Even though the audience can't see them, you can describe what you have in front of you. When speaking, think of your audience as people who are blind, which requires you to be very descriptive.

Radio call-in shows present a special challenge. If the questions are on point, and/or if you have a host who keeps the interview on track, calls can help you make your key points over and over. Even with "off-the-wall" questions, you will be helped if the host either screens the calls or helps you out by offering to bring the subject back to your topic. In the event of the bizarre or personal question, it's up to the person being interviewed to answer the question or topic and bridge to a topic that is of interest to all the members of the audience.

QUICK REFERENCE SUMMARY

- Media interviews are like presentations in question-and-answer format.
- Preparation is the key; have your selling points ready.
- Create an audience profile: Familiarize yourself with the program or publication, and *who they view as their audience*. If possible, get to know the interviewer's style and point of view.
- Keep in mind that your ultimate audience is those who watch, read, or listen to the interview.
- Remember, you are the expert, the "source." Your input is valuable; you can make the reporter look good.
- Take control whenever possible: Find out the topic and stick to it; set ground rules.

- Be on the alert for "tricky" questions. (Review the types in Chapter 11.)
- Learn the art of the graceful "No comment." (That is, never actually say "No comment," but offer an explanation for *why* you must decline to answer a question.)
- Never go "off the record." If you don't want to see it broadcast or in print, don't say it.
- Remember to bridge to your selling points.
- Learn the specific rules that apply to each type of interview.

Meetings, Meetings, Meetings

The one thing all business people know about meetings is that there are too many of them.

● ● ● ● ● ●

Generally, meetings are necessary when you need the input of several people, when a decision is required from a group, or when you need the synergy of group interaction, as in brainstorming.

● ● ● ● ● ●

You'll be wise to eliminate as many as possible by asking the key question: Is this meeting truly necessary? Perhaps a phone call, a letter, or an office visit would be more efficient or productive.

If the answer to this key question is no, or you're not sure, decide whether your meeting can be postponed or rescheduled, or your business handled in some other fashion. And as technology improves, another critical question for people in far-flung locations is: Do we all need to meet in person or will a videoconference work as well?

If the answer to the key question is yes, then you've got some preparation to do. Since you're this far in reading *Get to the Point*, you're already familiar with much of what you have to know. In this chapter, we'll discuss the similarities between meetings and other types of presentations and tell what else you'll need to know to conduct a successful meeting. (If you want specific rules for videoconference meetings, see Chapter 18.)

What *is* a successful meeting? In our experience, if you can discuss and take action on all of your agenda items and start and conclude on time, ninety-five times out of a hundred you can consider your meeting a success. It's the kind of success that enhances your value to your company or organization, the kind of success that gets you ahead.

PURPOSE, PLANNING, AND AGENDA

Once you have established the need for a meeting, it is up to you, the chairperson, to plan it or at least to supervise its planning. It is important for the purpose of the meeting to be clear. Presumably, since you carefully weighed the need for the meeting, its purpose is clear to you. Be sure it is equally clear to those who will be attending. You might want to give the meeting a title. When meeting announcements are sent out, a clear statement of purpose and/or a catchy title can focus attention on the objectives and help ensure good attendance.

* * * * * *

All meetings require an agenda.

* * * * * *

Agendas need not be set in stone, but without at least a loose structure, meetings wander. An agenda provides the chairperson a legitimate reason to move the meeting along.

If your meeting requires consensus on the agenda, you may want to reach agreement on a written agenda before the actual meeting takes place. This may mean preliminary phone calls, letters, or memos to solicit discussion items, opinions, and premeeting materials.

For more formal meetings, the agenda may include ground rules such as the length of time for opening statements and discussion, as well as rules for such issues as submission of materials and voting. Depending on the circumstances, even physical objects like tables can become items for discussion and even contention. Remember the Paris peace talks during the Vietnam War?

Usually you'll want attendees to have some sort of written agenda to refer to. If you don't distribute a sheet to each individual, put the agenda on a flip chart or a slide. At the very least, give an oral review before the meeting starts.

> **TIP:** *Whatever form your agenda takes, never include a minute-by-minute time schedule. It's fine to be organized, but meetings need a feeling of flexibility and you don't want a group of people constantly checking their wristwatches.*

Audience profile. Unlike any other presentation situation, the audience profile for a meeting begins with deciding who should be there. Sometimes these decisions are quite simple. It may be obvious whose input is needed to adequately discuss a given issue or problem. Often you will want to invite the entire marketing committee, or all the members of a particular organization. At other times, the decisions are more subjective and will reflect political concerns.

Once you have decided on the list of attendees, you should go through the standard audience profile. As we made clear in Chapter 2, while you wish to accomplish the agenda and basic tasks of the meeting, most people who attend the meeting will be judging it according to their *personal* question: What's In It For Me (WIIFM)?

Facilities planning. The goal of physical planning is to create an environment in which those attending your meeting can concentrate on the subject matter without undue distraction. A smooth-running meeting depends on coordinating all the elements in your presentation "theater." Basically, this means choosing the right room. The following considerations apply:

Size. The room should seat approximately the number of people you will bring together.

Seating arrangement. Depending on circumstances, different configurations of seating — table, theater style, amphitheater, or chevron — may be preferable.

Lighting. Aside from basic adequate lighting, the facilities should be capable of lighting the speaker well even while visuals are being presented.

Visual aids. Make sure the equipment you will need — overhead and slide projectors, flip chart, videotape players and monitors, and spares — will be available.

Amplification. If the room is large, check the public address system and microphone availability.

Lectern. If you need a lectern, make sure one is present.

Food and beverage. Make sure that there is room and equipment for any refreshments you are planning to serve, or that appropriate catering facilities are located nearby and have been notified.

Even with small meetings, it is important to do a little housecleaning and/or setting up beforehand. This may be as simple as cleaning up the coffee cups from the last group that used the conference room, or just tidying up and straightening the furniture and laying a photocopy of the meeting agenda at each place. Do something that says, "This is a serious working/communications environment; we appreciate your being here and will do all we can to make it a productive occasion."

Conference centers. To make sure that all these details are taken care of — without having to take care of them directly — many companies and organizations prefer to hold important meetings at conference centers, establishments that generally offer excellent facilities and can handle virtually any sized group. These centers are run by professionals who can provide valuable planning assistance. Just getting people away from the office and constant interruptions and phone calls may be worth the added expense.

A word of caution here, however: While conference centers generally provide excellent facilities, this is no substitute for doing your homework. You will still need to check out the meeting room, do a "tech" rehearsal, and practice with the equipment.

MEETING MANAGEMENT —
HANDLING THE INTERACTION

The entire tone of a meeting can be set by a strong opening statement. Opening statements should be short and to the point. Set yourself a time limit and stick to it.

If you want a model, think of a good opening statement you have heard in a political debate. At a meeting, the opening statement should always include a word of welcome, a review of the agenda, a statement of any ground rules you wish to establish, and the expected closing time.

❋ ❋ ❋ ❋ ❋

If the participants don't know each other, make introductions.

❋ ❋ ❋ ❋ ❋ ❋

This is an often-overlooked matter of protocol. In a small meeting you might ask participants to introduce themselves and perhaps to say a word or two on their expectations of the meeting. In a larger meeting, you should introduce the people who will be presenting.

Record keeping. Decide in advance what kind of records will be kept for the meeting. The chairperson should never be responsible for taking the official notes or minutes. In a small, informal meeting, you can ask for a volunteer. Usually, though, you should arrange beforehand for someone to serve as recording secretary. If you want a verbatim transcript, tape record the meeting. Most conference centers are set up to make full video transcripts of any meeting.

You may also want someone to list meeting items on a blackboard or flip chart. Appoint a separate person to fulfill this function.

⚜ ⚜ ⚜ ⚜ ⚜

In brainstorming meetings, record all suggestions, no matter how outlandish.

⚜ ⚜ ⚜ ⚜ ⚜

You can weed the list later on, but don't cut off suggestions unilaterally during the meeting.

Ground rules. Preestablished ground rules are vital to the orderly conduct of the discussion. Let the members know how much time is allotted to the overall discussion and how long each individual should expect to speak. If people run overtime, your job is to diplomatically cut them off. If Barbara Walters could cut off Presidential candidates during their televised debates, you should be able to enforce agreed-upon time limits for your discussion.

Summarize or offer clarifying comments from time to time during the discussion, as appropriate. This will often help to refocus a discussion that has wandered. Generally this commentary, along with your "parliamentary" functions, will constitute your contribution to the body of the discussion. (It is generally considered inappropriate for the leader to be a contributing participant in the substantive discussion.) If the agenda calls for a decision to be made, and it is clear that it cannot be made at the current meeting, the leader should make sure there is agreement on the next steps, such as whether the matter will be resolved by further correspondence and a follow-up vote by telephone, mail, or another meeting.

PEOPLE MANAGEMENT

Particularly in smaller meetings, personalities play an important role. We covered the common types of difficult questions and difficult questioners in Chapter 11. As promised there, we will now cover some additional personality types that sometimes create difficulties in meetings.

The Silent Type. Silence is usually golden, but meetings are an exception. In a meeting, you often want to build consensus. Other times, the opinion or contribution of a particular individual is crucial — especially when you know it will be voiced to others outside the meeting. That's when silence becomes a problem. Silent people are not necessarily unimportant people. In fact, the silence may be an expression of power. If you single out the silent type by explicitly requesting input on a given topic you risk intimidating or alienating this person. A better approach is to ask a question of the group collectively and then follow up by polling members individually, placing the silent person somewhere in the middle.

The Objectionist. This person sees the negative side of every issue, plan, or proposal. He or she is much like the Nitpicker or Detailer we discussed in Chapter 11. Don't confront this person during the meeting. A better approach is to present your ideas or objectives and seek consensus from this person prior to the actual meeting session. If the Objectionist tries to dominate your meeting, do not take this personally or show irritation. Offer to consider certain points and revert to the agreed-upon agenda.

The Monopolist. This personality bears some resemblance to the Objectionist but is not as negative. Like the Filibusterer we met in Chapter 11, this person just likes to talk and contribute, but finds it hard to come to the point. Enforcing time limits and being sure to elicit the opinions of others will help keep the Monopolist under control. "Henry, I'll get back to you in a moment. But let me first get the views of some of the other people who are here."

The Inadequate. The person who manifests the Inadequate personality may be vital to the group but, like the weakest performer on a sports team, needs support and a sense of belonging. Encourage this person to participate by helping him or her feel more adequate and powerful. Often, allowing this person to do small, easy-to-accomplish tasks will make him or her more productive at future meetings.

The Idealist. This person may be angry and belligerent or simply overly zealous about some cause peripheral to your meeting agenda. An effective leader will try to find common ground without necessarily subscribing to the idealist's full program. "Yes, this company does have many environmental concerns . . ."

DECISION TIME

When it is time to make decisions at a meeting, the chairperson is responsible for ensuring that the decision-making process is fair, efficient and accurate. Again, planning and advance preparation will make any vote taking easier. For internal meetings, the voting procedures are usually well established. For an external group, you should check the organizational or departmental rules, corporate bylaws, or constitution.

Other decisions include how voting should be done — by secret ballot, by voice, or by a show of hands — and whether the result should be determined by plurality, majority, two-thirds, or unanimous consent. Voice votes can generally be conducted by the chair. Be sure to ask someone to confirm your findings. A show of hands should be counted by two separate individuals. When you plan a secret ballot, prepare ballots in advance and plan a method for distributing and collecting them and counting the vote. Ballots should be rechecked and if necessary retained in a secure location.

CLOSING TIME

As the meeting winds down, people often begin to leave. At this point you need to take control. Often a clear statement of the remaining time and business will accomplish this. If you don't take control, the early departures will distract the rest of the attendees and often make them feel as if they are being kept after school.

❈ ❈ ❈ ❈ ❈

The closing of a meeting can be your most important moment in terms of input.

❈ ❈ ❈ ❈ ❈

The last things said in a meeting are remembered longest, so use your closing statement to stress the points you feel are most important. As with a more standard presentation, nearly all of your statement can be prepared in advance.

In addition to your observations, a good closing statement can include:

- A recap of important action items and decisions, so that all attendees leave with a sense of accomplishment and agreement (and will be more likely to attend future meetings).
- A general word of thanks for all who attended and special thank-you's to people who accomplished tasks, presented information, and took on responsibilities.
- A clear statement of when and where any follow-up meeting or event is to be held or, barring that, a statement of how people will be informed.

FOLLOW-UP

Meetings need follow-up, and this involves attention to details. As chairperson, you should always review the minutes before they are sent to the other attendees. Make sure the minutes are distributed. Also see that key commitments have been fulfilled. People sometimes make promises during a meeting and then delay or even fail to fulfill their promises. A polite note or phone call is often all it takes to do the trick. If this gentle prodding doesn't work, don't be afraid to use the legitimacy of the chairperson's position to encourage people to complete jobs they have undertaken.

Remember, if you have accomplished your agenda and have finished on or before your scheduled time, you can generally consider your meeting a success. Participants will consider their time well spent and they will be more willing to attend meetings you call in the future. Leading meetings effectively is a valuable skill that can lay a red carpet down the middle of your career path.

QUICK REFERENCE SUMMARY

- Key question: Is this meeting necessary, or will a call, memo, or one-on-one conversation accomplish my purpose?
- Meeting success criteria:
  — Start and end on time
  — Cover your agenda points
- Meeting planning checklist:
  — Audience profile
  — Agenda
  — Site preparation
  — Ground rules
  — Voting procedure
- Problem personalities to be prepared for:
  — *The Silent Type.* Don't confront this person directly. Rather, solicit input from each group member and include the silent member somewhere in the middle. — *The Objectionist.* If possible, seek consensus with this person before the meeting. If objections are raised *in* the meeting, offer to consider certain points and revert to the established agenda.
  — *The Monopolist.* Keep this well-meaning person under control by enforcing time limits and encouraging others to offer views.
  — *The Inadequate.* Encourage this person's participation by assigning him or her meaningful but manageable tasks.
  — *The Idealist.* The best way to deal with the missionary zeal of this meeting type is to find some common ground.
- Guide, clarify, and summarize as the meeting progresses.
- Make sure follow-up operations are carried out.

CHAPTER **18**

Picture Perfect Videoconferencing

In the 1960s, technologists promised us a futuristic device called the "Picture Phone." Well, 30 years later, the age of videoconferencing has arrived.

Standard videoconferencing of one-way video and two-way audio has become a reliable business tool. The next steps for business are dedicated two-way video rooms, portable systems, and soon-to-come desk-top video. Public rooms have sprung up where families can talk to each other, or prospective employers can talk to job applicants and save the cost of transportation to the home office.

• • • • • •

For the presenter, videoconferencing requires a unique combination of skills — presentation, meeting management, satellite media interviews, and graphics design.

A videoconferencing provider created a coffee mug with an illustration that describes the business need driving the technology. A harried executive is looking at his appointment book and moans: "New York at 8 a.m., Los Angeles at 10 a.m. No way." The coffee mug shows the solution. The executive sits in a video room and attends both meetings — first meeting with the group in New York, then connecting to L.A.

• • • • • •

As technology grows rapidly and costs decrease dramatically, more and more organizations are applying *interactive* videoconferencing. Why? Basic research from IBM indicates that people who see, hear and discuss a message retain 75 percent more than people who only read it.

That explains why meetings — if run well — are so important. That also explains the growth of videoconferencing. Videoconference pioneer, Peirce-Phelps, Inc., describes it as a **"timetool"** — a technology that saves time, reduces travel costs, boosts productivity, and improves decision making and business communications.

Interactive videoconferencing consists of two-way color video with voice and graphics capabilities. The clarity and detail of your images and production are very much a function of the type of transmission facilities you have purchased from a telecommunications (cable or telephone) company and the type of equipment you use.

For the presenter, videoconferencing offers:

- More active and frequent involvement with senior management (face time)
- Immediate information exchange
- Ready access to experts
- Faster access to information
- Ability to demonstrate skills for clear, focused, precise thinking

Here are a few ways major companies and organizations are using the technology:

- Corporations and associations have adapted the speakers bureau model and use videoconferencing to link up experts for key meetings. These are often two-way video with many graphics.
- Clothing manufacturers connect designers in the U.S. with factories in Asia. This allows for a clearer communications and can save time and expense in producing high-quality, finished garments.
- Multi-national pharmaceutical companies utilize videoconferencing to manage product development and communicate with regulatory agencies. The hope is that the technology improves communications and also speeds up decisions on drug approvals.
- Electronic speakers bureaus are created by videoconferencing. President Reagan was probably the first President to be "beamed in" to a meeting or convention. By President Clinton's administration, video presentation had become common for the President and many senior members of the administration. Usually this was one-way video and two-way audio.

Videoconferencing does not eliminate the need for in-person meetings. It does allow "face-to-face" communications when time is limited

or travel impractical. It is also often better than the standard conference call to prepare for the face-to-face meeting.

The applications are endless. Here are other ideas:

- Real estate agents for distant selling
- Telemedicine for connecting remote hospitals and emergency crews
  to experts
- Professional service companies for updates and planning meetings
- Freight companies for safety training

TIPS FOR EFFECTIVE VIDEOCONFERENCING

As with any communication medium, to be an effective video conference presenter, you have to not only be familiar with how the format
and its technology works, but how it can work best *for you.*

The basic premise, as with any presentation, is to **plan and prepare.**
The following tips will serve as guidelines for an effective video conference presentation.

Before the Conference

1. Familiarize yourself with the equipment, and how the cameras and
   screens are set up. Is there only one camera? Do you have a clear
   view of the screen(s)? Know how to:
   - Work the control panel
   - Pre-set the video camera positions
   - Use dual monitors
   - Work the microphone mute button and adjust button
   - Operate the document camera, and integrate video, slides and
     props
2. How sophisticated is the equipment? What bandwidth does it utilize? You need to know how you and your fellow conferees will look
   and sound.

   How sharp is the picture reproduction, especially in terms of any
   visual aids you plan to use? (FYI, the more bandwidth, the sharper
   the picture.)

   Beware of voice delays. Be prepared for the inconvenience of
   overlapping dialogue and long pauses.
3. Is it a one-on-one conference, a small group, or a multi-group/audi-
   ence conference? The size of the "field" will dictate how you choose
   to present; this will dictate your effectiveness.

4. Remember, television is a visual medium. Check seating arrangements. Make sure your attire is visually appropriate to the level of the conference.

   For men: Navy or gray, plain or pinstripe suit, light colored (but not white) shirts and solid/simple pattern ties.

   For women: A suit or dress, without fussy patterns, preferably one that doesn't reveal too much neck. Avoid all white, all black or all red attire. Keep hair carefully groomed; it should not fall into your face. Avoid loud jewelry — anything that moves or jingles.

5. Check sound acuity of microphone. Some are more sensitive than others — where one microphone may pick up the noise of papers being shuffled, another may not pick up your voice if you turn your head away. It can be somewhat disconcerting to watch a talking head with no voice.

6. If the meeting will involve more than two people and/or multiple sites, it is best to select a facilitator. Nothing is more disorganized than people at five different sites talking simultaneously.

7. Be aware that most equipment allows the participants to operate the cameras in both the Near End (where you are) and the Far End (the other location[s]). The facilitator should make sure the controls don't get "out of control."

8. Far more planning and a greater level of preparedness are needed for videoconferences, as they tend to be 20 to 30 percent shorter than standard meetings, and thus must be more focused and compact.

During the Videoconference

1. You will be seen almost entirely from the mid-chest upwards. Basic presentation techniques still apply.

   Body language is critically important — hands apart, shoulders relaxed, body leaning slightly forward, especially when the focus is on you.

   Watch quick movements. Moving while someone else is talking in your group is "upstaging." Avoid getting up and walking around when there is a critical presentation, as eyes tend to wander and people get distracted.

   Try to avoid side conversations; they are distracting, and project poor video conference etiquette. Those watching often feel they are being left out. Similarly, when you need to ask a question of a colleague at your site, you will need to ask him/her *through the eye of the camera*, for if you turn around to someone behind you, the other sites can't see what you are doing.

2. Video is a "close in" medium. Everything is highlighted, exaggerated. Time and space are condensed and amplified. Therefore, tone all gestures and movements down.

3. Be aware the camera can zoom, resulting in a tight close-up. Look alive and stay alert.

4. Remember, when you are speaking, the audience is watching a screen. Their attention may wander more easily. To engage their interest, make sure your information delivery is concise and effective.

5. When your group is on camera, direct your attention to the presenter if he/she is seated next to or in front of you. If the presenter is seated behind you, direct your attention to the camera. This helps maintain screen/audience focus on that presenter.

6. If presenting to an off-site group through a screen, look at the camera. If there is an ongoing dialogue on-site, direct your remarks to the person to whom you are talking. This keeps the conversational dialogue effect going. Beware, there is a tendency to be mesmerized by your own image on the on-site monitor. Also, keep in mind that if you use the monitor to check your hair or clothing, everyone else will see you doing this.

7. Learn companion technologies to show graphs and charts, but keep use modest. Some usage tips:
   - Large fonts, at least 24 point
   - Contrasting colors on plain paper
   - Large margins and landscape mode are essential
   - Remember the KISS rule for charts; bar slides and pie charts work well

8. Remember there are nuances with graphics and videoconference technology. The camera will pause for a second or two before switching focus from the speaker to the visual. Give the group time to absorb the visual information. The visual will also linger a bit before the camera switches back to the presenter.

Additional Reminders

1. Documents containing a lot of detail should be distributed before the conference.

2. Avoid shuffling papers or tapping objects near the microphone.

3. Consider distributing an agenda with clear goals for the meeting.
4. Introduce all participants.

QUICK REFERENCE SUMMARY

- Get to know your videoconference facility and learn how to use all the equipment.
- Become comfortable with the transmission quality. It's not quite broadcast.
- Observe videoconference etiquette. What works in face-to-face meetings may not be appropriate in videoconferencing.
- Learn the language of videoconferencing; i.e., you'll hear words like "codec," which simply means how equipment converts analog signals into digital and vice versa.
- The *Get to the Point* "Talking Memo" is an ideal format for preparing a videoconferencing presentation.
- Practice using graphics. Try the different techniques *before* the videoconference.
- The key to seamless videoconferencing is PRACTICE. It is a technology of the future, and managers will be judged in part by these communications skills.
- Videoconferencing can help businesses gain market share, increase the flow of products and services and hold down costs.

Being a Witness:
The Presentation That's All
Q & A

Being a witness — whether in a civil or criminal trial, before a congressional or legislative panel, at a regulatory hearing or an administrative proceeding — may be the most difficult communications environment you will ever encounter.

Why? The setting is often intimidating. The stakes are generally high. You're sworn to your testimony. Most of all, it's the questioner's forum, not the answerer's. So your ability to get your message across may be restricted.

Believe it or not, though, giving testimony is still basically a presentation, and with the proper preparation, you can maintain some degree of control and usually *Get to the Point.*

CASE STUDY: One of our clients was invited to appear at a congressional hearing on pharmaceutical pricing. There was a real question whether the company even wanted to send a representative, since it was anticipated that the hearing was going to be something of an inquisition. In addition, it was feared that the legislator sponsoring the hearing was not really investigating anything. Rather, he had already made up his mind and was merely using the hearing as a forum for making his points to his constituents and the media — very likely at the expense of our client. We were able, however, to convince management that, although it wouldn't be easy, such a hearing, properly handled, could be a valuable communications opportunity. The company decided to put in an appearance and make the best of it.

The best of it, of course, meant making some points of their own. The company president decided to testify, and he took our number one rule seriously. He prepared. As a result, he succeeded in communicating critical selling points about research and development costs, and about the economics of the business. A few of the more important comments were reflected in television and print coverage. As a result of his willingness to take the risks and then prepare properly, our client fared much better than the competition who shunned the hearing altogether.

Perhaps the main point to draw from this story is that, however difficult the witness stand may be as a communications forum, you should not be intimidated. There's always a way to prepare and make a point or two. Sometimes you can do quite a lot better than that.

Whatever your opinion might have been of the political actions of Oliver North, when he took the stand in the Iran-Contra hearings he was prepared and took advantage of the opportunities that arose.

Each type of witness environment — law court, legislative hearing, regulatory proceeding, investigative panel — has its own rules and procedures. If you're familiar with these, you can pretty accurately anticipate the restrictions you will be facing, and thus you can have a pretty good idea of the points you'll be likely to make. Let's look at each of these environments individually. *Caveat: If you ever find yourself in one of these legal environments, please consult a lawyer for the specific rules that apply to that setting.*

COURTS OF LAW

This is, of course, the scene most of us think of in connection with the notion of witnessing. While most of us have rarely if ever been in a courtroom, we have watched countless dramas on television and in the movies. In a sense, we all have a little preliminary training for this venue. It can be rather confusing, though, because in a real courtroom the story doesn't unfold in a smooth or natural way; it unfolds in pieces.

Trial testimony road map. Since the average television script doesn't take the trouble to explicitly set forth the rules of trial conduct, we shall give an overview here. Here's how the Q & A usually works: After jury selection (if any) and opening arguments, each side in the trial — prosecution (or plaintiff) and defense — calls its own witnesses.

Direct examination. The attorney for the prosecution or plaintiff calls witnesses for that side and conducts "direct examination." In the proper turn the attorney for the defense does likewise with defense witnesses. Direct examination is usually friendly questioning, in which your lawyer guides you through the unfolding of your story. "Please tell us, in your own words, what happened on the night of . . ." In other words, in "direct," you will usually be able to give full answers and get your selling points in, although a careful judge and skilled opposing counsel may keep your comments confined to the facts and will try to keep you from drawing conclusions and making judgments — which are part and parcel of good selling points. We suggest that you be prepared to try to get in as much of this information as possible. The jury can be instructed to disregard it, but having heard it, they can't entirely disregard it.

Cross-examination. The picture changes dramatically with cross-exam-ination. In "cross," the opposing attorney will have a chance to question you about your direct testimony. They will pick at details, and attempt to frame narrow questions that elicit a strict yes-or-no or other brief answer. You may have no idea what points the lawyer is trying to score. The main problem with cross-examination from the witness's point of view is that you rarely get a chance to explain or to repeat any of your story or selling points. A good lawyer will cut you off the instant you say the words *but* or *however.*

Our cross-examination advice is that you listen to each question carefully, and then *pause* for a moment before you answer. Pausing can be the most important tool of a witness. Pausing gives you time to think and gives your lawyer time to make an objection if necessary.

If you can't or don't want to answer yes or no, say so. A determined lawyer, however, may force you into a yes-or-no choice. In such a case try starting, "Although the answer is yes [or no] . . ." Your answer allows your qualification. Another tactic to consider is using the word *"and"* as a bridging device. If you can anticipate a question or issue in cross-examination, you can sometimes take advantage of a small opportunity to slip in information that is not directly responsive to the question. The examining attorney may ask to have it stricken from the record, but the jury will have heard it.

Coaching. A good lawyer will thoroughly prepare witnesses for both direct and cross-examination. When the stakes are high, this will involve careful rehearsal and videotape analysis. The film *The Verdict*, with Paul Newman, was not an accurate look at the workings of the law, but as an example of witness preparation it was superb. In a key scene, the defense attorney, played by James Mason, used videotape to prepare a physician for testimony. The firm staged a mock trial and let the witness see and hear what he sounded like. Direct testimony was rehearsed and the questions for cross-examination were anticipated.

If you ever have to testify in a trial, you should go through a drill for difficult questions, just as for any presentation. Keep in mind that in this situation you have a professional adversary — opposing counsel — who will search out any weaknesses in your testimony and probe them. So make your practices good ones. And make sure your lawyer is aware of all the tough questions you believe you will get. Your lawyer should then take you through the whole preparation process — direct and cross. If the stakes are high, this should include videotape feedback. As one lawyer we know put it, there should be no surprises from an opposing counsel, either on questions or on their witnesses' answers on cross-examination.

DEPOSITIONS

Although depositions almost always take place before an actual trial or regulatory hearing, we're sticking in a few words here. There are many reasons to have depositions. For your side, your lawyer wants to know what information the other side has. The other principle reason to have a deposition is to "make a record" in case a witness says something else at a trial. In this case, the deposition is used to "impeach" the character and veracity of a witness. Courts like to have depositions as part of the trial "discovery" process; if the parties find out as much as possible before an actual trial, they may be more likely to settle a case. Or at the very least, extensive pre-trial discovery may save the court's time in the actual trial.

No matter what the reason for the deposition, there are a few differences in deposition testimony versus a court room. First, very rarely do any of the body language and voice aspects of an actual presentation apply. A witness in a deposition can take as much time as he or she wants to answer. There is no need to worry about enthusiasm; in fact the flatter your voice tone, the better. However, witnesses should still remember to pause and think before they answer questions. They can also still ask a lawyer to clarify words they are not familiar with.

LEGISLATIVE HEARINGS

Legislative hearings are presumably held for the purpose of collecting information that will help legislators enact laws. In reality, they often serve other purposes, including providing publicity for individual legislators and their programs. In this sense, they are often "theater pieces," set up to realize a preexisting "script," and in which each witness is a sort of guest artist, playing a role.

There are rarely any surprises. Staff researchers have usually determined the positions of the witnesses beforehand, and thus the content of their testimony. This doesn't keep legislators from registering carefully rehearsed *expressions* of surprise for the television cameras.

In short, events at a legislative hearing are often staged and carefully choreographed for television coverage, down to details like choosing a room small enough that it will appear crowded even with only a few people present.

All this might lead us to the conclusion that testimony at such hearings is a pro forma affair at best. You appear to get on the record what the legislators already know, and answer questions, if they're asked. In keeping with what they understand these hearings to be, most companies and organizations prepare a written statement to enter into the record, and a chosen representative then reads a portion of the prepared remarks. It's all "for the record." In this boring situation, you will often find legislators reading their mail, talking to their aides, or working on other matters. No communication is taking place, and apparently no one *expects* any.

Our position is: Use legislative hearings as an opportunity, a chance to really make your points forcefully *and* dramatically in a public arena. As pointed out by Arthur Liman, chief counsel to the Senate in the Iran-Contra hearings, in criminal trials, "you sometimes leave the best story untold because of the rigid rules of evidence." However, in a congressional hearing, "you try to tell a full story so the American people know what happened and Congress can take appropriate corrective action."

So by all means appear. Let your words underscore the well-researched written position statements that you submit. Try to figure out how your company or organizational interests dovetail or coincide with those of the legislators (this is basic audience profile work). Find a way to play on the same side of the net — at least part of the time. Then dramatize your testimony. Think about vivid, visual selling points. Practice your delivery. You can make an impact.

REGULATORY PROCEEDINGS

Witness-stand testimony in this type of proceeding invariably follows pre-filed direct testimony. In other words, it is essentially cross-examination (with occasional redirect and recross), although compared to a court of law there is generally much more room for a witness to explain or amplify his or her answers. In light of this, many witnesses at regulatory hearings view their job as merely defending the written statement. Again, we take the view that such hearings, even though conducted on a cross-examination basis, are an opportunity to educate — and make points.

In practice, this means a lot of bridging. Preparation for a regulatory hearing should concentrate on the minus/plus analysis. The key bridges are areas where your company or organization shares concerns and issues with the public; it's the dovetailing principle again. It is also important to be clear about who your real audience is. Although you will be responding to the questions of a commission attorney or "intervenor," you may in fact ultimately be addressing the legislators' constituents, the public. During a regulatory hearing, often the most aggressive cross-examination comes from intervenors or "stakeholders" who are your business competitors. They **are not paid** to support your position. However, when the questioning gets difficult, don't take it personally. Lawyers surely don't. One defense attorney suggested to his witnesses that they think of themselves as *joint seekers after truth*. If you adopt that attitude, you will be less likely to get riled or make mistakes after getting angry.

SPECIAL POINTS FOR THE WITNESS STAND

Fundamentally, the rules for testimony presentations are the same as for more typical presentations, but often with a twist or qualification.

For example, it is essential that you know what you want to say and be prepared to say it forcefully, but as a witness you also need to be aware of how and when circumstances will make it possible for you to do so. That is, you need a clear understanding of the rules and procedures for information exchange and how these may restrict your ability to make your point. Above all, you should be prepared to bridge when you can, especially if you have reason to believe you will not be able to make your point without doing so. See your opportunities and take 'em.

You need to know your audience, but the audience you really wish to reach may not be the person or persons you actually address. In a trial, you are questioned by a lawyer, but you need to make your points to the jury or judge. In a legislative hearing, it is the legislature or the committee as a whole that you address, not the legislators or staff members holding the hearing. This audience can be expanded to include the public at large, through the media.

And of course all the basics of delivery apply here, too, only perhaps more so: Make good eye contact. Lean in when you answer questions; if there's a microphone, "embrace" it with your presence. Gesture with your hands and arms. Project and animate your voice. Keep your language simple; if you have to use technical language, industry jargon, or acronyms, explain them. Use signal words and phrases wherever possible. These are effective emphasizers, both as they are delivered and when written transcripts are reviewed.

The one overriding rule for all types of testimony is "Be prepared." It relates most clearly, perhaps, to the content and style of difficult questions.

CASE STUDY: Several years ago, we saw an important government witness reveal a weak spot in the context of a congressional hearing. Seated behind a table in the stately conference room, the senior official appeared relaxed and confident. He was handling questions well: His voice was strong and animated, he was leaning in to make his points, making effective gestures. Then on the next question, his whole demeanor stiffened: His voice flattened out; his hands went flat on the table. He answered the question, but his reaction clearly signaled that the legislator had hit a tender spot in his testimony. His reaction made the congressman continue to probe this area. Staff members made little checkmarks in the margins of their transcripts reminders to investigate this area further. So, while the witness didn't "say anything wrong," he still gave away the game.

You can take two steps to prevent this happening to you:

1. Anticipate all the tough questions and be waiting for them. Do the difficult questions drill and the Minus/Plus analysis; do them as thoroughly as you can.
2. Take our advice and pause before every answer you make. This way, whenever a question does take you by surprise, you have a little built-in recovery time.

Also, review the tricky question types we covered in Chapter 11. The one you're most likely to encounter in your witness role is the hypothetical. Be careful and methodical and qualify each hypothetical question with a phrase like, "That's an if question"; "In answer to your hypothetical question"; or "I'm continuing with your hypothetical line of questioning . . ."

The following are more specialized tips.

Listen. The full routine is five steps: listen, pause, think, reflect, answer. Experts can often be fast on the draw, anticipating the direction of a question. As you testify, keep in mind that there is a written record of the proceedings. If you listen to the entire question, you'll answer what is asked, not what you think is about to be asked. You will also make life easier for the court reporter or stenographer, who will not make as many mistakes and who will not have to stop you to slow you down.

Don't argue. This is for your attorney to do with the judge or hearing officer. You should try to remain calm and cooperative. But don't allow yourself to be trapped by a questioner's tactics, either. If you are asked a question that demands a yes-or-no answer and you can't answer that way, say so. If totally boxed in, try this response: "Although the answer is yes [or no], I would like to qualify . . ." With this tactic you have alerted those in the hearing room that you wish to qualify your answer and the written transcript will reflect this.

Be polite. When you take the stand, take the trouble to say "Good morning" or "Good afternoon" or some other civilized pleasantry. Try to be conversational in your responses, no matter how rigorous the questioning gets. Jurors tend to believe witnesses who are likable.

Flag the hypotheticals. On the witness stand, it's appropriate to call attention to hypothetical or "if" type questions. Unlike a general presentation or media interview, responses that we covered in Chapter 11, on the witness stand, particularly if you're an "expert" witness, you may be forced to answer such questions.

Our suggestion is that each time you are forced to answer a hypothetical question, start your answer with a phrase like: "Well, counselor, in answer to your hypothetical . . ." or "In answer to your speculative question . . ." or "In response to your supposition, let me state . . ." Make sure that if the follow-up question continues the hypothetical premise, that you continue to flag the answer. The result will be a signal to the questioner and the court that you are being a careful witness, you will continue to think clearly, and most importantly the written transcript will be very clear as to the nature of the questions and the responses.

Be prepared for the media. The news media, particularly the trade press, are usually aware of public and administrative hearings. Reporters may approach you for a statement. Review the suggestions in the "Quick Reference Summary" for Chapter 16. In particular, avoid saying "No comment." Give them at least a general selling point statement that reiterates the major elements of your testimony.

Bring a "crib sheet." Prepare a card or sheet with three or four of the points you want to make at any regulatory or legislative hearing. (These are not allowed in a court of law.) It's like the plus side of the Minus/Plus Worksheet.

We learned this lesson from a woman who testifies frequently in public utilities hearings. She is well qualified, being an accountant and a lawyer. And she is always well prepared. She always brings a sheet of paper summarizing the points she wants to communicate. On one occasion, an attorney noticed that the witness kept referring to her notes. (Keep in mind here that anything you bring to the witness stand is "discoverable" and can be introduced into the record.) The attorney swooped down on her accusingly: "You appear to be referring to a piece of paper that I do not have. What is it? We would like to have it introduced into the record; please tell us what it is."

Without skipping a beat, the witness responded, "Sure, counselor. The paper contains some of the points I wanted to communicate here today. One of them is . . ." And before he could cut her off, she had scored one of her points. A great example of taking advantage of your opportunities.

Two final thoughts we'd like to leave with you. The first is an idea we got from another seasoned witness: Treat the experience like a job interview. Think about it. When you go for a job interview, you must be positive; you must think about the points you want to get across; you have to anticipate the questions, answer them, and bridge to positive information; you must be enthusiastic and sell yourself. All these points apply to the witness.

The second thought is one of our themes and a suggestion that often turns the experience around for people who are dreading it: Have a good time!

QUICK REFERENCE SUMMARY

Sworn testimony can be the most intimidating of all presentation settings because it's the questioner's forum — and frequently an adversarial situation. However, with proper preparation, you can usually maintain enough control to make your point.

Court of Law
- The rules of evidence would seem to make it tough to make *your* points, especially on cross-examination.
- The attorney for "your" side should rehearse you thoroughly and should give you the opportunity to make all the points you feel are important.
- In cross-examination, be prepared for all "difficult questions." Have answers.
- Anticipating the line of questioning in cross-examination can help you to score points.
- You can sometimes be forced to answer hypothetical questions on cross-examination. Always be sure to qualify your answers: "In answer to your hypothetical question . . ." or "If I must speculate, I would say . . ."

Legislative Hearings

- Although often pro forma, legislative hearings provide an opportunity for *you* to make your points, often to a very large audience.
- Live testimony generally supplements presubmitted written testimony.
- Often, you are given wide scope to make your own statement. Take advantage of this: Prepare. Have strong selling points. Practice your delivery.
- Remember that your audience is "the people."

Regulatory Proceedings

- Witness-stand testimony in regulatory hearings almost invariably follows pre-filed direct testimony. Hence it is, in essence, cross-examination.
- Hearings, however, do not run under strict rules of evidence. As a witness you have a wide range of opportunities to make your point *by means of bridging*.

For All Types of Testimony

Know what you want to say and be prepared to say it forcefully. Remember, it is almost never the person asking the questions who is the ultimate audience of your communication. In a trial it is the judge or jury. In a legislative or regulatory hearing, it is generally the public.

- All the rules of delivery apply to testimony: Gesture; keep your voice animated; make eye contact, especially with cameras.
- As with all Q & A, remember: Listen, Think (which also means "pause"), Answer.

The Job Interview

The job interview is the ultimate one-on-one selling presentation. Given two candidates with equal credentials on paper, the better presenter or communicator will almost always get the job.

● ● ● ● ● ●

Job interviews involve virtually all the main elements of presentation making.

● ● ● ● ● ●

Included are the audience profile, content preparation, selling points, preparation for difficult questions, bridging — and practice. And depending on the job, even visual aids may come into the picture.

Your goal for the job interview, as for any presentation, is to be focused, prepared, and positive. One important thing to keep in mind about this presentation is that although it is billed as an interview — which suggests that potential employers ask the questions and you give the answers — it's actually an interactive event, a two-way process. You're there so the hiring company can find out about you; you're also there to find out about the company, the position, and the people in the company.

Although you should certainly plan on asking questions at the interview, don't wait until then to begin gathering information about the company. Do your own audience profile, as you would for any presentation. This is important for three reasons:

1. It makes sense for you to gather as much information about the organization and the position as you can so you can judge whether this is the right situation for you.

2. Personnel officers and recruiters tend to be favorably impressed by the thoroughness and foresight demonstrated by a candidate's having researched the position in advance. It makes you look good.
3. If you do like what you see, then like any audience profile, your research helps you create more "audience-centered" messages. If you really understand what the organization is like, you can stress the ways you fit in with it.

It is generally not difficult to gather relevant information about a company, even a specific position. Corporate annual reports, stock and brokerage analysis reports, electronic data bases, trade and consumer articles, and former employees are all viable sources of information. Perhaps more specifically helpful will be the executive recruiter (if any) who told you about the job and your own personal network of friends and associates. If you can't get information any other way, call the company public relations or investor relations department and ask for some background.

Try to get a basic job description, including responsibilities and salary. Other key areas of advance information relate to the management and decision-making style of the department you would be joining and the personalities of the key managers. If, for example, you are a real go-getter being interviewed for a position in a department with a very laid-back management style, you should be aware of this and have some idea of why they would want to hire you.

※ ※ ※ ※ ※ ※

You already have a list of your personal selling points. It's called your resume.

※ ※ ※ ※ ※ ※

The accomplishments you list there are the headlines; the specifics will be provided by you during the interview. Your preparation should include pulling together at least one strong anecdote or other specific for every point you have listed. If you can come up with two or three, you'll look that much stronger. Try to make your selling points as visual as possible; let the interviewer see the examples in his or her mind's eye.

THEIR QUESTIONS

Preparing for a job interview is similar to preparing for any other question-and-answer session. Keep in mind that in this case the questioner is an official representative of the organization you hope to work for and that the basic message you want to communicate is the corporate or organizational WIIFM: What's in it for us to hire you? What's the significance of your accomplishments and experiences for *this job?*

Those are the questions to keep at the back of your mind as you make out your Difficult Questions Worksheet and your Minus/Plus Worksheet. With some reflection, you should be able to anticipate virtually all the questions the interviewer will ask. Naturally, this will include questions about your past work history, which may well contain some tender spots you would prefer not to have someone probe. In other words, like any presentation, the job interview is likely to involve questions you would prefer not to answer. And, as in any presentation, you will need to be prepared to deal with them: Respond to the question and bridge to more positive information.

In addition to questions you'd rather not answer, you need to be alert to the other types of tricky questions we covered in Chapter 11, particularly hypotheticals. Job interviews frequently involve speculative or hypothetical questions of the type, "Where do you see yourself ten years from now?" or "If you were running this division, given this set of facts, how would you respond?" You are almost required to answer these. Just flag them as hypotheticals before you do so. (*Note:* The question "Would you be willing to relocate?" may not be hypothetical.)

What you don't have to say. Lest we leave you with the impression that you are at the mercy of all the interviewer's questions, be assured that there are questions you shouldn't feel obligated to answer.

As always, personal questions fit into this category. With the rising concern over individual rights, some of these areas of personal information have been declared off limits by law. This doesn't always stop interviewers from asking the questions, however. The best policy is to be polite and state firmly that the question is personal and can have no bearing on your work performance. If necessary, negotiate a little and offer other information that may be relevant.

Example:

Question: *"Do you plan to have children?"*

Answer: *"Can you explain why that is relevant to this interview?"*
or "I don't see how that is relevant, but if you're concerned about my commitment . . ."

You should also avoid answering questions that delve into proprietary information relating to your present position. Sometimes these questions are posed in an effort to gain information, sometimes just to test your reaction — since most employers don't want to hire somebody who's ready to give away information. Don't fall into this trap; just politely decline to reveal proprietary information and suggest that they would be unhappy if their employees did so in the course of job interviews they might have.

Some questions that come up in job interviews are just plain dumb. These could be anything from "Who do you think will win the World Series?" to "What did you think of that ugly sculpture in the lobby?" We suggest that you resist any impulse to be flippant or sarcastic. just answer the questions, and treat them as a way for you to make another point (i.e., bridge to another selling point).

TIP: *Don't bad mouth present or previous employers.*

YOUR QUESTIONS

Your audience profile and research probably won't answer all your questions about the job and company, and the interview is the time to ask them. We suggest you prepare a list of questions or points that you wish to bring up. Realistically, there are a lot of things you *should* find out about. Some of your questions may just confirm information you gathered elsewhere. Having the list with you doesn't obligate you to ask all the questions on it, but the notes will be living proof of your preparedness. It's not unlike going to the doctor's office with a list of symptoms, concerns, and questions. In the pressure of the moment we tend to forget, and a list helps us remember.

Try to spend time with people you will work with, not just with the interviewers and people you will report to. These meetings will fill in your perspective on the job and the company.

DEMEANOR AND DEPORTMENT

All of the skills we discussed in the core of the book apply equally to job interviews — only more so, since the stakes are higher. The impressions you make are crucial, from your clothes to the way you walk in and greet the interviewer to the way you sit, gesture, make eye contact, and use your voice.

- Good eye contact is crucial. Let your gaze rest on the interviewer's face rather than letting your eyes roll skyward or look down at the floor.
- Remember to **pause** before answering questions (see pages 107–110).
- Lean in to answer questions.
- Show your enthusiasm. Enthusiasm, or at least a good energy level, is important for any interview. Don't be a corporate cheerleader, but let your interviewer know you are capable and have an energetic, positive attitude.

SPECIFIC JOB INTERVIEW TIPS

Drinks. If your interview involves going out for a meal, you may have to decide whether or not to have a drink. This question is less likely to be a test of character than in days past. If you are inclined to have a drink, you may wish to follow the lead of your hosts: Do if they do, don't if they don't. On the other hand, it is also becoming more socially acceptable *not* to drink, so if you are inclined not to, don't. If the drink is a rite of passage or congratulatory gesture, on the other hand, it is best to go along.

Warmups. Clients tell us their best interviews are the ones where they are a little relaxed. (Not totally relaxed; a bit of adrenaline is helpful.) You may want to find the time and place to do the kind of relaxation warmup we recommended in Chapter 13.

Decisions. Try to be clear about your motives in attending any given job interview. Is this really a job you want? Or are you just testing the waters, checking opportunities, or simply strengthening your job interview skills? Don't get tense over an interview for a job you don't really want and then agonize if the job is offered — or if it isn't.

Visuals. For some kinds of jobs — advertising, public relations, or design, for example — it may be appropriate for you to bring samples of your work such as ads or press releases. If you do bring samples, please remember our cardinal rule about the presentation of visuals: If you have preliminary remarks or explanations, make them. Then present the visual — and pause — long enough for the material to be absorbed and evaluated.

QUICK REFERENCE SUMMARY

- Job interviews should be interactive and conversational.
- Do an audience profile on the company or organization.
- Be prepared to relate the selling points on your resume to the objectives and outlook of the organization for which you are interviewing.
- Prepare for Q & A with the Minus/Plus and Difficult Questions Worksheets.
- Practice bridging to your selling points.
- Always ask questions.
- Be aware of your body language, eye contact, and energy.
- Send follow-up and thank-you notes with specific references to your conversations.
- Study the industry, not just the company.

How to Prepare and Read a Speech

We feel that delivering a speech from notes is almost always preferable to using a fully prepared text. With notes, your eyes aren't glued to words on paper. Your performance has more spontaneity and you can look at the audience. Nonetheless you may at some time feel the need to work from a prepared text. Some of the occasions when you will want a prepared speech are: when the rules for all presenters are the same, when copies of the talk will be distributed to attendees, more formal events such as annual meetings, very precise introductions, an explanation of rules and procedures, or if you don't have the time to rewrite the prepared speech from the company speech writers into your own words and thoughts. Here are some guidelines that will help you maintain eye contact and generally enliven your speech.

TYPING THE SPEECH

Use large fonts/type. Print your speeches with a large enough font so it's easy to read. Most of our clients prefer standard writing, with normal upper and lower case printing; others like all uppercase letters with key initial letters slightly larger.

(For those with more primitive technology, most electric typewriters and daisy wheel computer printers have an element (daisy wheel or type ball) available for just this task. The typeface is often named something like "Orator." Most dot matrix printers can print double height and/ or double width characters. If possible, use the double height, double width combination.)

Type phrases, not lines. Divide each sentence into thought or meaning units, then type only one thought or phrase per line. Double or triple space between lines. For example, the beginning of Lincoln's Gettysburg Address would become:

FOURSCORE AND SEVEN YEARS AGO
OUR FOREFATHERS BROUGHT FORTH
    ON THIS CONTINENT
A NEW NATION
CONCEIVED IN LIBERTY
AND DEDICATED TO THE PROPOSITION
THAT ALL MEN ARE CREATED EQUAL.

Use only two-thirds of the page. Leave at least the bottom one-third of the page blank. If you fill the page, by the time you read to the bottom, you are looking down at quite a sharp angle. This tends to make your voice drop and certainly makes eye contact difficult. Leaving the bottom blank also reduces text density, making it easier for your eye to pick up words and phrases. In combination with the improved reading angle, this encourages you to make eye contact.

Don't jump paragraphs. Always try to finish a paragraph on the same page on which you started it. This eliminates confusion as you move to the following page; you'll have a natural pausing point and can give yourself ample time to move the page and continue.

Number pages. Clearly.

FINE-TUNING THE SPEECH

Mark up your text. Read your speech aloud, listening for the points where you will want to pause, emphasize words, and group words together. You can use the markup signs found in Chapter 12 on page 151. Consider using colored pens to make your notations extra legible. Be neat.

Pauses: Put a slash (/) after a completed thought or sentence. Use a double slash (//) when changing thoughts or for dramatic impact.

Emphasis: <u>Underline</u> words to be emphasized. For extra emphasis, use double underlines. Generally, *emotional* and *action* words get this treatment.

Joining: Use a connecting line ⌒ to join words that should flow together and be spoken in one breath.

Here's how our example might look, marked up for delivery:

> FOURSCORE AND SEVEN YEARS AGO /
> OUR FOREFATHERS <u>BROUGHT FORTH</u>
>   ON THIS CONTINENT
> A <u>NEW</u> NATION //
> CONCEIVED IN <u>LIBERTY</u> /
>
> AND <u>DEDICATED</u> TO THE PROPOSITION
> THAT ALL MEN // ARE CREATED <u>EQUAL</u>.

Make marginal notes. At the beginning of your speech — and wherever you need reminders — give yourself marginal instructions such as "SMILE," "GESTURE," and "SLOW DOWN." Some people prefer symbols: A stick figure might mean "gesture"; upward or downward arrows could serve as inflection cues; eye glasses for eye contact. Use whatever works for you.

Don't staple pages. When delivering your talk, lay your pages on the lectern and move the first page to the left of the pile. As you finish reading the first page, reach with your left hand and move the second page to the left, on top of the first page. Continue in the same fashion. This is something like the way a page turner handles the problem for a musical performer. The idea is what's coming is important, not what's past.

Pause. Use pauses liberally in your talk. As we've said at every opportunity, pauses give your audience time to digest and appreciate what you've said. Pausing also gives you reading time, so you can then look up and make eye contact with the audience as you begin each new paragraph.

Practice, practice, practice! Generally, do a *minimum* of three runthroughs — out loud, with a tape or video recorder and/or an audience. Listen for clarity of phrasing and good vocal inflection. For the full story on practice, see Chapter 12. See also the section on lectern techniques, in Chapter 15.

QUICK REFERENCE SUMMARY

- Type your speech in large type or all capital letters.
- Type in phrases, not sentences or paragraphs.
- Mark your script with symbols to help you with pace and inflection.
- Practice, practice, practice.

Using a Teleprompter

The teleprompter is a standard tool for delivering a speech on television or videotape. It has also become the preferred method for reading a speech to large groups of people. In many ways it is ideal, since it enables you to read text while you appear to be looking at the audience or looking directly into the camera.

But the benefits of the teleprompter can be liabilities as well. Because you are reading text, you can easily forget about your audience and not look up. For the television-mounted devices where there is no audience present, it is difficult to maintain the energy and enthusiasm you would bring to a live audience when speaking from notes. A speech on a teleprompter is still a speech — the presenter has to work hard to make it conversational and connect to the audience. Hence these guidelines.

THE MACHINERY

Basically, there are two types of teleprompters: One is a video monitor, usually placed over the camera lens, to which a copy of your text is transmitted. The other consists of one or two flat glass screens — placed to the left and right of a lectern. This is called the Presidential or Outrider Teleprompter and is suited to speaking before live audiences such as large corporate meetings, product launches or political conventions. In older models, a printed text is rolled through a machine as a video camera transmits the text to the screen or monitor. In most newer models, the speech is sent directly from a computer to the reading screens.

REMEMBER THE BASICS

Although you will be reading from glass panels or speaking to a camera lens, remember that you are addressing an audience — either just past the glass or through the camera. Before a live audience, the tele-prompter can be an advantage over a "hard text" since it forces you to look up a bit more than just reading from a lectern.

＊ ＊ ＊ ＊ ＊

A speech delivered from a teleprompter is still a communication. Remember to be concerned about how it is received by the audience, not just how it is delivered.

＊ ＊ ＊ ＊ ＊ ＊

Use pauses liberally to give your audience time to digest and appreciate what you've said. Gesture to burn off tension and animate your voice. Look up as if reading a regular speech to make eye contact with the audience. With the TV-mounted machine, maintain eye contact with the camera to avoid looking uncomfortable or insincere. If possible, make notes on your text or put an easel stand next to the prompter with notes reminding you to "SMILE," "GESTURE," and "PAUSE."

For the Presidential or Outrider prompter, we recommend that like any other speech, that you memorize the opening and closing paragraphs. Know the speech well enough so you can look up and make strong eye contact.

PREPARE YOUR TEXT FOR A TELEPROMPTER

Type and mark your script just as we described for a live speech except that you may, of course, use the whole page. The problems of reading angle and eye contact have been eliminated by the technology.

Get Comfortable

Do as much as you can to make yourself at home. Arrive early at the presentation facility or studio. Get to know the technicians and crew. As President Clinton discovered the hard way when he made his first major healthcare speech to Congress, you should make sure that your speech is correctly loaded into the computer or hard-copy prompter.

With the outrider model, know your speech well enough to be able to go from one glass to another, usually at the end of a thought or sentence. Make sure you adjust the angle of the glass so it's easy to read.

* * * * * *

Always bring a hard copy of your speech in case the technology malfunctions.

* * * * * *

When you're in a studio looking at a camera, you want to appear as if you're talking to a real audience. There are several of ways to do this:

- Visualize someone behind the lens whom you know or want to know, and talk to that person.
- Actually talk to the technician behind the camera, or have someone stand next to the camera who you can talk to.
- Bring a picture of someone you know — your kids, a loved one, your dog, whatever works for you — and tape it next to the camera lens or prompter screen to help you relax.

Mentally recreate another setting in which you have given your speech.

CASE STUDY: This last approach worked well on one occasion when we were coaching an executive who was new to the videotape process and the studio atmosphere.

He was a few minutes into his speech and it frankly wasn't going very well. He was stiff, wooden, and flat. We stopped him. "Where did you originally give this speech?" we asked. "Colorado Springs," he told us, "at a sales meeting." "All right;" we said, "we want you to put yourself back there in that sales meeting." As soon as his mind returned to that setting, his reading became very natural, as if he were talking to that audience and not to the camera. The rest of the taping went beautifully.

* * * * * *

The cardinal rule to remember with teleprompters is lead, don't follow!

* * * * * *

Whatever the type of prompter, there will be an operator whose job is to adjust the flow of copy to accommodate your reading pace. Remember that you set the pace; don't ever feel that you have to wait for the copy, or have to keep up with its flow.

What You'll See

About six lines of copy will be visible on the screen at one time. As you read, the text will scroll upward, revealing the next lines. *Again, set your own pace. You drive the system, it shouldn't drive you.*

PRACTICE

We've said it earlier in this book; we've said it elsewhere; we say it again. With television, it's more important than ever. You are about to be a classic "talking head." Which means that your audience is going to be listening — and watching — close up. If at all possible, practice with videotape, in a studio. If this is not possible, use an audio recorder and practice in front of a mirror, or have someone observe you and comment on your performance — or both. Listen carefully to be certain your sentences are not too long to be easily understood. Generally, at least three out-loud rehearsals will be required before you will begin to feel comfortable with your speech.

When you use the Presidential teleprompter, the audience can see the screens in the room and generally has higher expectations for your talk. Since you're using expensive technology, they will expect you to be a better communicator.

If you think it doesn't take practice to deliver a speech, consider the case of one actress who did more than one hundred "takes" of her role in a television commercial before she was satisfied with the reading. Her lines? Just two words!

QUICK REFERENCE SUMMARY

- Lead the teleprompter, don't follow.
- Relate to the audience through the camera lens or by looking up from the screens.
- Visualize a real audience or real presentation situation, or create a substitute to speak to, either a real person or a picture of someone.

Give and Take: The Panel Discussion

As a communications environment, the panel discussion offers a nice mix of elements. It's more spontaneous than a speech or one-on-one interview. It is inherently interactive and offers both audience and participants the stimulation of an immediate contrast of views. The environment can be adversarial, though not to the extent that a trial or hearing is, so this too can be stimulating.

In a panel discussion you know your speaking time will be limited — but you have no way of knowing how limited. Hence panelist profile preparation is critical. In order to have the best chance of getting your points in, you must anticipate opposing positions and arguments:

- For ease of reference, list your key points on a five-by-seven index card.
- Always be ready to bridge.
- Also, be ready to jump in and make your points based on other panelists' statements.
- Try to repeat your key message two or three times during the course of the discussion.

THE SPLIT AUDIENCE FACTOR

One factor that complicates the preparation process for panels is that you're dealing with a "split" audience. This creates an unusual amount of audience profile work.

On one hand, there is your "true" audience, the people in the auditorium or those who are watching or listening to the broadcast. These are the people you're trying to sell your points to, so you'll need to do the normal audience profile: Get a firm understanding of who they are and center your messages on their concerns and their awareness (WIIFM).

On the other hand, you can't forget the moderator and the other panelists, the people with whom you will be interacting directly. Realistically, you're not there to convince them or win them over to your point of view, but you must be ready to respond to the issues and points of view they will raise, to anticipate the challenges they will present. To be effective, you need to know who's going to be there and what their areas of expertise are, along with their points of view and prejudices. So, given all of these players — audience, moderator, and other panelists — and the time constraints, set realistic, limited objectives. Concentrate on a few important selling points that you'll have on your note cards.

Here are a number of techniques and tactics that will help you make your point in panel discussions.

What to Find Out Ahead of Time
- Know the themes and sub-themes of the event. How is it being billed or promoted?
- Who is the moderator? What is his or her perspective and/or agenda?
- Will you have an opportunity to make an opening and/or closing statement? Always make these statements, if at all possible.
- What is the physical environment — the panel setup, microphones, water pitchers, audience seating? If you can influence the seating arrangement, get yourself located at one end of the table. These are the "seats of power."
- Can you appear with a colleague? It's usually more effective if two people can represent the same organization.
- Can you bring handouts, brochures, or other reading material to leave with the audience? If you can, this is an excellent way to reinforce your message.

At the Panel
- Arrive early. Introduce yourself to the moderator and the other panelists. If not prearranged, find the best seating positions.
- Set up any charts or other visual aids you have brought (after first making sure this is appropriate).
- Take a few moments to relax before the panel begins. Stretch and limber your muscles and your voice (see pages 159–161).

- Review your key points just before things get under way. Keep your note card in front of you during the proceedings. Take a few deep breaths just before it is your turn to speak (see page 155, Chapter 13).

During the Discussion

- Be sure to address the audience, not the panelists, during your opening and closing statements.
- Sit up and lean slightly forward when you speak. This demonstrates energy and commitment — and allows for better breathing.
- When others talk, keep your eyes on them. When responding to another panelist, begin your answer by looking at him or her, then shift your eye contact to the audience. This includes them in your answer, reduces the likelihood of a rebuttal from the panelist, and cues you to bridge your answer to an issue of interest to the entire group.
- Don't try to control the course of the discussion, but be sure to jump into the dialogue at any appropriate point and bridge to your selling points. If a colleague is appearing with you, decide in advance which of you will address which issues and which of you will take on the responsibility of responding to unfocused questions or those not directly in your area of expertise. It's important not to look confused or unprepared.
- Most important, be constantly on the lookout for opportunities to add your points when your colleague or another panelist has finished talking. Unless strict rules of order have been set up, you don't have to wait your turn. If you have an important point that addresses the audience's needs, try to make it. Signal the moderator with a hand gesture or use a word or two to make a natural transition. Key words to use: "I'd like to add . . ." or "From our perspective . . ." or "Here's another point . . ."
- When your colleague/co-panelist is talking, your job is to think of selling points or specifics that drive home the general answer. This ability to have both of you answer shows a team approach and helps build audience retention of your message.
- Keep your sense of humor. Don't take comments personally, particularly in an adversarial discussion. Enjoy the opportunity to deliver a message to an audience.

After the Panel

- Make yourself available for informal conversation with members of the audience.
- Leave reading material or handouts with a contact telephone number or address so interested persons can reach you.
- Tell the panel organizers that, subject to your schedule, you are willing to appear at other discussions.
- To evaluate your own performance (as a guide to possible improvement for future panels), check your note card or other list of crucial points. How many of your selling points did you get in? Did you get your key message across two or three times?

QUICK REFERENCE SUMMARY

- Prepare for two audiences: the listeners, and the moderator and other panelists. You want, ultimately, to communicate to the first, but you must do so by addressing the second.
- Keep your objectives limited; concentrate on a few important points.
- Jump in after other panelists' points and bridge to your message.
- Don't be afraid to repeat yourself. Try to make your key point two or three times.

How to Introduce a Speaker

Introducing a speaker is one of those jobs that doesn't get much attention — if it's done right. It's when it is done badly that everyone notices.

An introduction is a mini-presentation, with its own shape and choreography, and as such contains most of the elements that by now should be familiar. In fact, the only presentation elements that don't come up are the Q & A and visuals.

AUDIENCE PROFILE

Like any presenter, to prepare a good introduction you need to know the audience. Generally, you already do. If not, you need to do enough of a profile to understand what about the speaker will appeal to them. You are the connecting link between audience and speaker.

YOUR MESSAGE

Essentially, your bottom line message is, "Here's a great speaker." Your selling points are details about his or her background, qualifications, current activities — whatever compelling information you can gather to pull the audience in. Your call to action will be something like, "Please join me in giving a rousing welcome to So-and-So."

⊕ ⊕ ⊕ ⊕ ⊕ ⊕

The speaker's name should usually be the very last words out of your mouth.

⊕ ⊕ ⊕ ⊕ ⊕ ⊕

Here's why. First, it's your show only until you pronounce the name; then the audience's attention goes instantly and directly to the speaker.

Once that transition occurs, you no longer have an audience. Second, the speaker generally takes his or her name as the cue to get up and walk to the lectern. A premature introduction can cause considerable confusion and embarrassment.

In addition, saving the speaker's name until last sometimes adds a bit of suspense — a touch of showmanship that is actually not out of place in an introduction. Why showmanship? In one sense, as an introducer you have a function similar to the warmup band at a rock concert or the kickoff person at a political rally. Unless the speaker is famous or well-known to everyone, you are there to generate enthusiasm for what follows.

Beginning
To create enthusiasm you need to start with a high level of energy. The first words out of your mouth tend to set the tone. Accordingly, a good grabber is particularly important in introductions. Much of what we said earlier about grabbers (see Chapter 5) applies here, except that personal connections established should be between speaker and audience. Humor is a good ingredient if it comes naturally to you and is not inappropriate in terms of subject matter or occasion. Current events often provide a meaningful tie-in.

Middle
The main body of the introduction consists of information about the speaker (selling points) that will whet the audience's appetite. Social rules require us to be modest about ourselves in public, so your job as an introducer is to be *immodest* on behalf of the speaker, just as you would be about your company's product; hype his or her accomplishments, credentials, and stature. Like any other presenter, you're there to make a sale, to sell the speaker to the audience.

Selling Points
All too often, "introducers" limit their selling points to a thumbnail biography accompanied by a dry list of books and papers written, titles and degrees earned, affiliations, and/or other credentials that reveal very little about the person involved. The more you can convey a sense of knowing the person, however, the better you motivate the audience to do the same. This kind of connectedness comes from mentioning personal involvements, current projects and activities, something about

the contents of books or papers. In fact, another device that often adds a touch of suspense is to foreshadow some aspect of what the speaker is actually going to say. Find out what the speaker is going to say and set up the talk without stealing his or her thunder.

As with all selling points, try to illustrate facts about the speaker and information about his or her work and accomplishments in dramatic terms. This means translating your points into words and images the audience can relate to intuitively. Your linking task becomes much easier if you have an opportunity to talk with the speaker beforehand, so take the time to get to know the speaker if you can. If you don't get a chance to speak about *anything else,* check the factual accuracy of all your information with the speaker before the event. It is embarrassing to all when the speaker feels compelled to correct academic or professional background information.

Ending

Once you've finished your remarks, deliver your call to action: "Please join me in welcoming . . ." If applause is appropriate, lead the applause. At this point, you have two options. You can leave the speaker's platform, which is often the simplest logistical choice, or you can stay to physically welcome and "install" the speaker. If you choose to stay, you will need to *step back* as the speaker nears the lectern, to let him or her pass in front of you. Generally, you will shake hands and "turn over" the lectern. Once he or she gets settled in, you will probably get a word or two of thanks, which is your cue to quickly exit.

As with any presentation, the more preparation and practice you put in, the more successful the introduction will be.

AWARDS CHOREOGRAPHY

If the occasion is an awards ceremony, the person performing the introduction will generally be the one to physically present the award. In some circumstances, especially where a number of awards are being given, you may want to keep your remarks quite brief. In other cases, especially where only one recipient is to be honored, you will probably want to speak at greater length. When you have concluded your remarks and announce the recipient's name, you will step back, holding *the award* in your left hand, shake hands with the recipient when he or she arrives, hand over the award, and depart unobtrusively.

QUICK REFERENCE SUMMARY

- Remember that you're the link between the speaker and the audience.
- Find personal notes, relevant anecdotes, or a WIIFM (What's In It For Me) message in addition to the standard listing of honors and accomplishments.
- Save the speaker's name for last.

CHAPTER **25**

Quick Points:
Presentation on a Time Budget

#1: THE INSTANT PRESENTATION

The setting: An elevator, at the water cooler, leaving the cafeteria, at your desk.

The situation: A boss or peer stops you or phones you and demands an on-the-spot opinion, evaluation, update, or progress report. The need: A clear, concise, convincing thirty-second response. The strategy: Listen, Think, Answer.

Step 1: Pause. That's right; pause. At all costs, resist the temptation to engage your mouth and let it drive the brain.

Step 2: Think. Who is this person? What's his or her relationship to me? What is his or her concern or relationship to the issue raised?

What is the most succinct, bottom-line-oriented message I can deliver in a relaxed, conversational manner?

Is there a specific fact or example that supports my message?

Step 3: Answer. Deliver your statement with the most conviction and confidence you can muster.

Step 4: Follow up and close. Don't be upset if you can't answer any follow-up questions that may be forthcoming. Try to answer them, but don't let the impromptu encounter go on too long. You can excuse yourself with a remark like, "I'm on my way to an important meeting . . ."; "You've caught me in the middle of something that can't wait"; or "I've got someone sitting in my office . . ." Generally, it is prudent to

241

offer to fulfill the request at your earliest convenience: "When would you need the rest of this information? I'll put it together for you . . ." whenever.

The instant presentation occasionally turns into a longer conversation. But focus on the first thirty seconds. If the encounter does run longer, try to develop a good closing line before you break it off.

#2: THE TWO-MINUTE TALKING MEMO

It happens all the time in business: You've been asked to make a presentation — sometimes couched as an "update" or a "status or progress report" — in your boss's office or at a staff meeting in ten minutes.

Here are guidelines that will enable you to pull off this assignment with style.

Put this kind of a presentation together the way you typically read a memo (as opposed to the way memos are usually *written*): *Get straight to the bottom line.*

You do this by determining and delivering *the information that this person or group really needs to know.*

Here's the simple, four-step technique:

1. Write your bottom-line message first. (This is the same as the information this person or group really needs to know.) It should consist of no more than two or three sentences.
2. Pull out two or three essential facts, or pieces of data that support or prove your conclusion or bottom line. As you select your supporting points, consider how they support the conclusion. Ask yourself the questions: "So what?"; "Who cares?"; "What's the significance of this fact or data?"
3. Write a strong opening for your two-minute talk. This opening could be a relevant anecdote or personal note, a prop that helps people visualize your point.

   Example: "If we increase production and authorize overtime, we can reduce our two-week back-order problem." This avoids the more standard (and boring) opening: "I want to give you an update on our order situation. . . ."

4. Review your material. Make sure you can deliver the basic message in two minutes or less. Anticipate any questions.

When you actually deliver your talking memo, the elements appear in the following order:

1. Opening
2. Bottom-line message, if different from the opening
3. Supporting points
4. Bottom line message — again — as conclusion message

#3: "IN-FLIGHT" PRESENTATION WRITING

Here's a game plan for making the most of your time when you have to prepare a presentation in a limited — but not severely limited — amount of time (for instance, on the flight from Kansas City to Seattle). It is really an expansion of Quick Point #2, bridging the gap between the real shorties and a full-fledged presentation, adding the possibility of visuals, more and clearer selling points, and more time for Q & A.

Tools required are an airplane (or other) seat, a note pad, and a pen or pencil.

Audience profile. As in a full-length presentation, the first step is taking stock of who will be there. If you know the people, visualize them. What is each person's role in the proceedings, each person's personal concern? Who are likely to be supporters of your position? Who are likely to be opponents? What are the personality types? What "What's In It For Me" message can you formulate for each person or position represented within the group you will be presenting to? Jot down this information on your pad.

Your roles and goals. Using your audience profile, make a quick mental review of the stated reason for your appearance in this presentation setting. This should help you assess the basic expectations of those you will be addressing. In other words, what's your role here? Next, jot down a simple, clear statement of what your message is in the presentation:

- Consensus?
- Data?
- Ideas?
- A Sale?

(The object of this segment of preparation is to make sure your messages are both audience- and speaker-centered.)

Gee whiz points. What new, startling, amusing, unusual, or thought-provoking fact, statistic, or anecdote can you use to get the attention of your listeners and/or dramatically illustrate your selling points?

Problem-solution sheet. On one side of your page, quickly list all the problems, challenges, or negative aspects of your subject that occur to you. Don't worry about ordering or ranking them. Across from the negative points, list all the solutions, recommendations, or positive selling points that come to mind.

Identify your key issue. Look over your list of solutions and recommendations and pick the one that best keys in to the WIIFM needs of your audience. This is your key audience-centered issue. Your task is now to link it firmly to your personal bottom-line message with one or more strong bridges. This is the core of your presentation.

As with all bottom-line messages, you will state your positive point at the outset. Then you will examine the problem or negative. Finally, you will restate the solution or recommendation. (Tell 'em, tell 'em, tell 'em.)

Minus/Plus Sheet. Using your problem-solution sheet as a guide, make a real Minus/Plus Worksheet, listing every possible negative question or issue that might come up in the context of your talk, and indicate bridges to positive information. Make sure you have a bridge and a positive answer for every negative point on your sheet. Study your Minus/Plus Worksheet and rehearse your bridges.

Select visuals. Look over your material and decide what points would make good visuals. (In this scenario, you need to think in terms of flip chart visuals, since there is no time to create slides or overheads.)

Notes. Make notes if you feel you will need them. Keep them concise. List details and specifics, not general principles.

Run-through. If you have an opportunity (in the cab ride from the airport, for example), rehearse your talk — out loud. Spend some time visualizing tough questions, and practice bridging from these to your selling points.